Happy
to Help

LESSONS LEARNED SERVING
ONE MILLION CUSTOMERS

Happy to Help

LESSONS LEARNED SERVING
ONE MILLION CUSTOMERS

JESSE B. GOOD

Library of Congress Cataloging-in-Publication Data

Good, Jesse B
    Happy to Help! Lessons Learned Serving One Million Customers / Good, Jesse B
    p. cm.
    ISBN-13:978-1545141199 (Jesse B Good Publishing)

Printed by CreateSpace, An Amazon.com Company
Book layout and design: Orange Pulp Graphic Design & Web Design
www.orangepulpgraphics.com

More information on Happy to Help! and Jesse B. Good, go to JesseBGood.com

For my wife—

Lacy

—who is always happy to help.

Table of Contents

INTRODUCTION

Customer Relationships trump everything. With twenty-five years of front-line, customer-facing background, and having served over one million customers, this is the most important thing I have learned; that customer relationships are paramount. Cultivating a lasting loyal business relationship with your customer pays off better than the best marketing, advertising, or promotion. It's an interesting dichotomy, because the reason to operate a business is to make money. However, when money becomes the primary focus, the relationship suffers. Conversely, when the focus is on building the relationship, an increase in revenue becomes a direct byproduct. When a service provider's intent changes to building relationships, they truly become "Happy to Help" any and every customer.

Good Family Relationships

My grandfather returned home to Wyoming after serving in the Navy during World War II. He homesteaded land and went into the work he had grown up with—farming. As a worker in an agricultural business, relationships were extremely important to him. As a farmer, he often spent time at the John Deere dealership. They not only knew him, but they knew his tractors.

On one occasion, he sent my grandmother to pick up a replacement part. When the young man asked her which tractor it was for, she responded, "The green one." Despite the fact that all John Deere tractors are green, they were still able to help replace the necessary part, as they knew which tractors my grandfather owned. The people at John Deere were not concerned about taking my grandmother's money. They were successful because they maintained a personal customer relationship.[1]

One of my first jobs in college was working in a video store. There were only ten or twelve employees who worked there, as we were a smaller location with a small community to serve. We all became very close and enjoyed working with each other. When the general manager of the store decided to pursue a career change that would allow him to work more daytime hours, it was an emotional affair.

We had a small meeting and going away party. I remember him saying with tears in his eyes, "You guys are all like family to me. Really. I spend more time with you than I do my own family." While he was speaking to us, his coworkers, I believe that some of those heartfelt relationships had also been built with our customers. It is for this reason I refer to customers as a customer family rather than a customer base, or a database of customers. Those terms are all about numbers; real customer service is about relationships.

At the time of this writing, we are quickly approaching Thanksgiving. This brings mixed emotions for me. Thanksgiving is equated to time with family. While there are family members that I am excited about seeing, there are others I would be just fine to not see at all. I'm willing to bet that you can relate. Isn't it funny how some of the people who drive us the craziest are family? Yet, the people we enjoy the most, have the strongest relationships with, and consider to be our closest confidants, we say are "like family."

I've been treated like family from service providers who genuinely cared about me, and were concerned about my needs being met. I've been able to treat customers like family and build relationships with them. Once, my team and I even held a surprise party for a customer, and everyone chipped in to buy him a birthday gift. Real customer service, real experiences, real marketing or sales is all about creating relationships. According to sales expert, Jeffrey Gitomer, the number one reason people purchase is because they like their sales rep (or organization).[2]

DTR – Defining the Relationship

Customer service is a term of familiarity, along with its younger brother (newer concept), *customer experience*. These terms are quite different, though many people use them interchangeably. They can best be designated with the following scenario:

1. While driving down the highway you see a billboard for a new restaurant. At work the next day, a coworker tells you about how great the new restaurant is. You decide to try out the new restaurant and invite a friend or significant other to attend with you. A few days later you pick up your companion to go to the new restaurant.

2. As you arrive, you navigate your way through a crowded parking lot, but find a parking stall that you feel is a reasonable distance from the front door. The two of you walk toward the restaurant and comment on the large fountain in front of the restaurant. Once you enter, you observe that the entryway is covered with colorful flowers.

3. When you approach the front kiosk, you are greeted by a friendly hostess who promptly seats you.

4. After a few seconds, a server approaches and takes your order. He is nice, friendly, and well-groomed. He smiles, tells appropriate jokes, and is prompt with everything that you order.

5. After your meal, you walk back through the flower-covered entry, past the fountain, and back to your car in the parking lot. You comment with your companion about what an enjoyable experience you had.

6. A few weeks later, you decide to take the same companion back to the restaurant, and have an equally enjoyable experience on your second visit.

7. You begin enjoying the restaurant so much that you begin calling them your "favorite" and recommending them to all of your friends.

Customer service is the most granular portion of this scenario. It is specific to the instances that you interacted with, or were served by another person. Specifically it includes parts 3 and 4. It may be referred to as a *customer service experience*, but does not include the elements of a full *customer experience*.

The *customer experience* includes every part that pertains to a singular visit, and is not limited to people. In this case the first experience includes what happened between points 2 and 5. Point 6 would be a second and different experience, but would include all the elements of the first experience (points 2 through 5).

Customer relationships begin from the first contact with the organization, in this case point 1. The reason relationships with your customers are so important is because they continue through point 7 and beyond as long as that relationship is maintained.

Now that I've ranted about the importance of relationships, I get to tell you that you're reading a book that focuses solely on *customer service*. While customer service is the most granular and a smaller portion of the overall experience, the value of this small portion outweighs the rest. No matter how beautiful the fountain or the flowers, no one will return to your business if your customer service sucks. On the other hand, many businesses do just fine without the bells and whistles (or flowers and fountains) because their customer service is fantastic. It is desirable to offer a great experience, but customer relationships cannot exist without delivering great service.

This book details lessons I've learned from delivering newspapers at age eleven, through twenty-five years of experience in restaurants (fast and casual), call centers, retail (including Black Friday), a number of hospitality and entertainment venues, and up to facilitating more than one million customer service experiences.

Reno

Recently, my friend, Reese, and I went to lunch at an Applebee's and received one of the most pleasant dining experiences of our lives. As we entered the restaurant, we were greeted by a friendly hostess who showed us to our seats. She was happy to accommodate our request to sit at a bar table. In just a few seconds, our server arrived. He introduced himself as Reno and asked to take our drink order. I asked for a 7-Up and Reese ordered a root beer. Reno was off in a flash and quickly returned and asked if we were ready to order our food.

Reese ordered first. "I'll have a Cowboy Burger with extra onion rings and extra barbecue sauce." Then he looked at me.

"I would like the Clubhouse Grill without tomatoes and extra honey barbecue on the side," I added. We noticed that Reno wasn't writing down our order.

"Would you guys like an appetizer to start with?" Reno asked.

"Yes," I replied. "Let's get the buffalo wings. And can we just get those plain with the sauce on the side?"

"Sure," Reno replied without hesitation. "What kind of sauce would you like?"

Reese and I debated for a moment than asked for barbecue sauce, hot sauce, and ranch dressing. With that, Reno was off to get our order into the kitchen.

In a few moments, Reno brought us our appetizer exactly as we had ordered. As we began eating our wings, Reese finished his drink, set it on the table, and commented to me how important it was to him that his drink stay full.

"I have a hard time leaving a good tip for a server who can't keep my drink full. I even stiffed a guy one time because he didn't bring me a single refill." He reached down to pick up the empty glass for emphasis but to his surprise, Reno had already replaced his empty glass with a full one.

Not long after, our entrées arrived. Like our appetizer, our entrées arrived exactly as we had ordered. Reno worked to give us flawless service throughout, and we were pleased with the experience.

A couple of weeks later, Reese and I contemplated what we

wanted to eat for lunch. Because we had such a good experience previously, we decided to return to Applebee's. The same friendly hostess was working, and asked if we wanted to sit in Reno's section. Our response was, of course, a resounding, "YES!" Reno was pretty amazing that first time around, but he blew our minds on this visit.

Normally, when a server approaches your table for the first time, the first thing they ask for is your drink order. Not Reno. When he arrived at our table, he held my 7-Up in one hand and Reese's root beer in the other—the same drinks we had ordered on our one previous visit. We were amazed and thrilled.

Quincy

During a period of unemployment, I found myself spending a lot of time at Office Depot. I discovered that Quincy, who managed the print department, was the best printer in town. In those days, resumes and cover letters were not sent electronically as often as they are now. Most of the positions I was applying for still required that the resume be delivered in person or sent via the post office.

I never explained to Quincy that I was unemployed and desperately looking for work, but I'm sure she figured it out. She gave me a card that allowed me student discounted pricing even though I was no longer a student. She knew my paper stock preference and even knew which folder on my disc to access to print my documents. I would walk into the store, hand her my disc, and she would load the printer with the right paper and ask how many copies I needed.

If I needed more than one copy, she would always print just one to make sure it was correct. If, for whatever reason, it didn't look right, she would throw it away and wouldn't charge me for it. She made great recommendations for me and did whatever she could to help me be successful. When I finally found employment, several months went by before I returned to Office Depot and saw Quincy. When I did see her again, she was quick to ask how I was and how the new job was going. She was fantastic!

Gordon

A year after purchasing our new home, my wife and I decided it was time to start making some modifications. The first thing to go was some shrubbery in our back yard. We agreed that the space would make a better flower bed. Lacking the necessary tools for the job, I went to Lowe's to make some purchases.

I was fortunate to meet Gordon. Gordon worked in the lawn and garden section and was an immense help. He asked specific questions about what I was trying to accomplish, and then helped me find all of the tools I needed to get it done.

A year later, when it was time to replace our lawn mower, Lowe's was the first place I looked. Fortunately, Gordon was still working there and was ready to help me. He explained all of my options and helped me figure out which mower would be best for our hilly terrain. He even provided instruction about the little package of oil that was included with my mower purchase. Gordon explained that I needed to be careful as I wouldn't actually need the entire pouch. I would need to use most of it and just leave about a pinch in the pouch.

Sure enough, when I returned home to start my new mower, Gordon's instructions were perfect. I used his suggested portion of oil and things went incredibly smooth. I was extremely impressed with his detailed instruction and assistance.

Now, there is a small hardware store about a mile from my home and Home Depot is about six miles away. Yet, I drive more than ten miles to Lowe's because I know Gordon will take care of me. To date, Gordon has sold me a lawn mower, edger, pick-ax, a barbecue, and a handful of garden tools. Although Gordon only works the lawn and garden section, his incredible service has lead me to make additional purchases at Lowe's including a refrigerator, freezer, and a washer/dryer set.

Customer Service

You've heard stories like these before, and if you're lucky, you've been served by people like Reno, Quincy, and Gordon. These are all service providers that are happy to help. What you may not realize is how exceptional they really are. Even in organizations where customer service is the norm, finding employees who consistently do a great job can be unusual.

A study by Forrester Research found that while eighty percent of businesses believe they offer "superior" customer service, only eight percent of their customers agree.[3] How can this be? Why is there such a gap between what businesses and customers perceive as superior service?

This is likely due to the "5-90-5 Rule." As Ari Weinzwig explains, only about five percent of employees are customer service superstars that rarely (if ever) require training. On the opposite end of the spectrum, you will find the bottom five percent who just won't figure it out no matter what you do. They are just not meant to work with people. In the middle, where most of us live, is the ninety percent. These are the people who have a desire to offer great service, but require guidance and training to move to the skill level of the top five percent.[4]

This is where the problem lies. Most organizations don't offer formal customer service training during the on-boarding process. Employers often believe that if they hire for personality and train the skills, they will just find and hire those top-five percenters—this is rarely the case. When those employers hire one or two employees who do offer stellar customer service, they tend to believe that everyone in their organization offers that high level of service. What they don't realize is that technique is important too. No matter someone's personality, if they don't have communication skills, critical thinking tools, or the ability to smile at people, they won't succeed.[5]

I've had other servers at Applebee's, and while there are one or two that are almost as good as Reno, most are average. Similarly, I've worked with other employees at Office Depot and Lowe's that try to be helpful, but I've had others avoid eye contact at all costs. Few measure up to Quincy and Gordon. It seems clear that if customer service training were offered to all employees at each of these businesses, *most* employees should perform at nearly the same level (let's not forget that bottom five percent).

Regarding my own experience in customer service, I admit that I have not always served like a top five-percenter. While I felt successful as a paperboy, a cook at Wendy's, and a DJ at a roller skating rink, the truth is that I was still just a ninety-percenter. Sometimes I was a really awesome ninety-percenter, and other times, I was more like the bottom five-percent. I've given bad service. I've done stupid and mean things to people who annoyed me.

For example, I used to work in a facility that had a video game arcade. We closed the facility at 11:00 p.m. during the week. On more than one occasion, that time approached and passed, but there were a few customers who still had coins and continued to play. At about 11:05 p.m., I turned off all the breakers and shut down the arcade completely. Pretty awful, right?

This is where most businesses are. They hire people they think will do a great job, but don't offer training outside of processes, policies, and systems that are specific to the business. If you aren't training your employees, then you are leaving them to their preprogrammed skill levels.

Training

What do great customer service companies like Disney, Starbucks, and American Express have in common? They all understand the value of deliberately and consistently training their employees in delivering great customer service. It is no secret that these companies spend marginally more time on training employees' customer specific skills, yet very few businesses follow suit.

Personally, all but one of the jobs I've held were customer facing positions. Of these, not one offered me training to build relationships or create better service experiences for my customers. In contrast, a good friend of mine who worked at Disney World as a Merchantainment Hostess, spent three days in training before ever coming into contact with a customer. Do you know what a Merchantainment Hostess is outside of Disney World? A cashier. Yes, she spent three days in training, learning job specific skills as well as customer service specific skills before working with a single customer.

I have worked with organizations that have cashiers working the cash register and interacting with customers the very first day. For one business, cashiers were at the cash register within the first hour. It's hard to offer customer service specific training when managers are so anxious to get employees trained on a cash register.

I understand that very often the first thing that comes to mind when I mention training is budget. I am often asked, especially by small business owners, "How can I afford to?" My reply is, "How can you afford not to?"

What is Customer Service?

As a hiring manager I often asked applicants, "How do you define customer service?" I could ask that question a hundred times and get a hundred different answers. Most of them were acceptable, but there was no common definition or plan for performance. One girl simply said, "Duh! It's serving the customer!"

As I began studying more about customer service, I found that there are multitudes of books extolling the virtues and the importance of offering great service. However, I had difficulty finding a specific definition for customer service. After years of serving customers and studying best practices, I created my own definition of what customer service looks like, and was able to narrow down training great customer service to three specific steps.

The bulk of this book is devoted to better understanding and implementing these steps. The best part is, you can begin using these steps to improve your customer service today!

The first step is to *Discover*. *Discover* your customer's needs by *engaging* them in casual conversation. *Enquire* about what need you can fulfill specifically and why they chose you over a competitor. As you learn about their needs, *enlighten* them about your product, services, or purchasing procedures to create smoother experiences.

The next step is to *Deliver*. *Delivering* effectively requires three important skills. First, you must *Deliver exactly* as your customer requested. Second, *Deliver elegantly* by being a genuinely polite, pleasant, and nice person that utilizes good manners. Use the kind words your mother tried to teach you like *please*, *thank you*, and *you're welcome*. Third, *Deliver energetically* by being happy, friendly, and enthusiastic. Show people that you enjoy your work and are ecstatic about the opportunity to work with them.

The third step is to *Do More*. *Do More* by going the extra mile for your customer to *exceed expectations*. You can offer *extras* to your customer like rewarding them for being loyal, getting to know them on a personal level, or sending them a thank you card once in a while. Part of *Doing More* is to continually *evaluate* your own customer service performance and seek to improve those skills.

Let's be clear about why customer service is a performance. Customer Service is sometimes a department you call when you have a problem with a provider. Or it may be where you go to return clothing that doesn't fit. Customer Service is also something that employees do when they interact with the people who purchase from their business. In this case it is a performance.

Once I began training the concepts of *Discover, Deliver, Do More*, I saw dramatic performance improvement. It wasn't just about the customers either. Managers began treating employees better. Employees began treating each other better. And everyone began treating the customers better.

Here's why this works: *Discover, Deliver, Do More* gives everyone a common definition of what customer service is, as well as a plan for executing it. And, as the skill level of service providers improved, everyone's personal desire improved, making them happy to help. Here are some of the results I've seen from implementing this training in various businesses:

- An entertainment venue saw increases in purchasing of every attraction leading to an overall growth of twenty-one percent in annual revenue.
- One company focused on improving a specific three-hour period of each day. A few weeks after training, revenue during that same three-hour period had increased by almost eighty percent.

- At one organization, *Discover, Deliver, Do More* was used to create a word-of-mouth marketing campaign during the slower months of business. The year prior, the organization spent over twenty thousand dollars on one advertising campaign. It was a flop. They penetrated less than one percent of the target market and each dollar spent on advertising brought in about nine cents in revenue. When this organization focused on building word-of-mouth, the only cost was for training. Every dollar spent on training was tracked to bring in about six dollars. The return on investment was sixty-seven times more effective than the advertising campaign that failed the previous year.

Where We're Going

The chapters that follow take a deep dive into the steps of *Discover, Deliver, Do More*. Each chapter features real life stories of good and bad customer service. We'll discuss the subset of skills required to be successful with each step. There are also practical examples, review questions, and exercises that can be done with a partner or team. Finally, I've included some challenges for comparing your organization to the competition and some pictures that fit the theme of each chapter.

After learning more about the three main steps, we'll explore how you can use these same steps to create Service Resolution when there are gaps in your customer service performance. I'll also leave you with some quick tips for improving service performance.

Zappo's CEO, Tony Hsieh, has said, "We don't look at customer service as an expense, we look at it as an extension of our marketing budget."[6] Indeed, taking time to train your employees with customer service skills is a valuable investment.

When you maximize your customer service performance, you:

- ❏ **Ensure customer happiness and retention** (the first most effective way to grow business is also the most cost efficient; do not lose your existing customers[7])
- ❏ **Increase spending with each transaction** (the second most effective way to grow your business and also the second most cost efficient; higher per capita spending from each customer[8])
- ❏ **Accelerate the frequency of purchasing** (the third most effective way to grow business and the third most cost effective; higher repeat business from your existing customers[9])
- ❏ **Multiply your customers' personal recommendations** (the most effective and cost efficient way to gain new customers; ninety-two percent of consumers believe recommendations from friends and family over all forms of advertsing[10])
- ❏ **Experience an expanded and thriving customer family** (the result of the four previous points combined)
- ❏ **Continuously cultivate lasting loyal business relationships** (perpetuate the cycle by creating and growing relationships with customers, old and new alike)

Let's get started!

DISCOVER

Alex pressed "Print" on his computer only to see the notification he hated most. His printer was out of toner. He had an important project due at work that day he desperately needed to print it. He resolved that he would stop by an office store on his way to work that had a print shop. While it would certainly make him arrive at work late, it would ensure that his project would be delivered on time.

When Alex entered the store, he saw one employee at the cash register ringing up a customer. Near the back of the store, in the computer section, he saw another employee also helping a potential buyer. He made his way over to the print counter and waited . . .

And waited . . .

And waited . . .

And waited . . .

After several minutes passed, he began looking around to see if help would be arriving shortly, if at all. The employee in the computer section began helping somebody else with writing utensils, and now a second person was waiting in line at the cash register. He began to grow increasingly impatient, especially since the whole idea of coming to this store was to deliver his project on time.

Finally, Alex saw an employee approaching the print desk. The employee walked behind the counter of the printing area, worked on the computer for a minute, and then walked away, without even acknowledging Alex's existence.

Alex checked the time on his cell phone and noted that he had been waiting nearly ten minutes. He paused for a moment to consider his options. At the top of his list was driving across the street to a competitor. While it could potentially save time if someone was available to print his project immediately, he considered the time that would be lost trying to get through traffic at the busy intersection.

Alex resolved that he would wait two more minutes, and if he was not helped by then, he would make his way to the competitor across the street. Fortunately, only a few more seconds passed before an employee finally arrived at the print desk and was ready to help Alex with his project.[1]

Have you ever been in this frustrating situation? Sadly, it isn't exclusive to office supply stores. You've probably been through this when you have you been put on hold for an outrageous amount of time ordering a pizza. Or, when you had to call your cell phone carrier about an issue with your phone and were put on hold. Or, maybe you were told someone would contact you within twenty-four hours only to have to call back after going three days with no response. Or, like Alex, it happens to you in person, when you have to stare down an employee who is too busy to help you because they are talking with their co-workers or sending a text.

Alex's story is an example of the first step of building relationships with customer service performance:

Discover what your customer needs

This first step is the foundation upon which the other two steps will be built. Without this one, the others are impossible. As can be seen from Alex's example, many businesses miss the opportunity to adequately *Discover* the needs of their customer, to the point that the customer is prepared to buy from a competitor.

As easy as working with a customer seems, there are a lot of moving parts. The reasons an employee may not effectively *Discover* the needs of a customer vary, but they are almost always one of three things:

1. *They don't know how to engage a customer.* It's no surprise that our skills in interpersonal communication have changed. Technology has made it so that we can interact with almost anyone at any time or place—and not always verbally. Having spent a fair portion of my life working in entertainment, I'm no stranger to seeing people on dates. One of the saddest and oddest things I have ever seen is people on dates that don't even talk to each other, instead spending the majority of their time on electronic devices. If you're not

27

even interested in interaction with a date, what hope do you have of interacting with your customer?

2. *They don't know how to find out what a customer wants.* Many jobs out there teach employees to ask, "Would you like fries with that?" Or, to say nothing at all while wearing a vest that says, "How can I help you?" When employees do speak with you, they ask things like, "Can I help you?" to which the answer will almost always be, "No, I'm just looking." If you don't know how to ask the right questions, how can you find out what your customer needs?

3. *They are unclear about how to set expectations for the customer.* Many times, a customer service provider is just one small piece in a larger puzzle. When there is potential for a problem further down the line, customers usually won't find out about it until it is too late. This may be due to apathy or ignorance on the part of the customer service provider. Regardless, any foreseeable issue should be brought to the attention of the customer. How can you expect to create a loyal customer relationship if your customer never knows what to expect from you?

The solution to each of these three problems lies with helping employees understand how to effectively *Discover* the needs of a customer. There are three specific skills associated with this step of *Discovering* your customer's needs. The first skill is to *engage* the customer in friendly conversation. The next skill is to *enquire* about your customer's needs. The final skill is to *enlighten* them about any concerns that they may have as they purchase.

Engage

Lacy went to do her household shopping at a local outlet of

a national retail store. She selected the items she needed to purchase, and then entered the checkout line. She put her purchases on the small conveyor and waited as her items moved closer to the clerk. She was surprised that he didn't say hello or even look-up, but just started sliding her items across the scanner.

Beep.

Beep.

Beep.

Lacy kept her eyes fixed on him waiting for some sort of greeting. After scanning all of the items, he stopped and looked at her, but still said nothing. She stared at him, waiting to hear the total for her purchase . . . and waited . . . and waited. When she finally realized he wasn't going to say anything, she asked, "How much is my total?"

Still not saying a word, and with an annoyed look on his face, the man pointed to the small display that showed how much she owed for her purchase. She gave him the money and, again, without saying a word, he handed her the receipt with her change and began checking out the next person.[2]

Did you notice that he did not say a single word during the whole transaction? He didn't even make a sound, let alone smile. How is that for *engaging* a customer? Do you think he was happy to help? He didn't even talk to her. Sadly, this is a national chain which employs over one million people in the United States alone. You would think a chain this successful should at the very least be able to effectively offer some level of customer service. Think again.

Engaging your customer requires that you acknowledge their existence. It can be difficult when work gets busy. Maybe you find yourself understaffed and having to deal with several people at one time. At least make the effort to smile at someone who is waiting and let them know that you will help them as soon as you can.

If you work in the office, the same can be true for email communication. While you might not be able to fulfill someone's request right away, it only takes a few seconds to send a brief message letting them know you are working on their request.

If you can't help them because some other daunting task requires all of your attention, let them know that, too. Don't just walk behind a kiosk, desk, or other barrier, fiddle on the computer, and then walk away. Acknowledge their existence with a warm, "Hello!" or, "Welcome to Jesse's Place! I'll be with you in just one moment." There is no excuse for not acknowledging your customer.

When you are able to get to the next customer, you can really improve the interaction by thanking them for waiting. A lot of people apologize for the wait, but I suggest that you don't apologize for an inevitable wait that you had no way of avoiding. (Like that customer who spends an exorbitant amount of time in line looking for a coupon, or when there wasn't enough meat on the grill to service everyone's order.)

Apologize when you have done something wrong or there has been a service gap and you are sincerely sorry about your error. If it's busy and your manager didn't schedule enough people, or someone called in sick, this is not your fault. And, are you *really* sorry? Probably not. It's just a formality we've learned from people that stink at customer service performance.

Save the apologies for when they are really needed and when you really mean them. (Like when the customer's order was made wrong because you rang it up incorrectly.) Just thank them for their patience. I contest that a friendly, "Thanks so much for waiting," or, "I really appreciate your patience," will go a lot farther than an insincere, habitual apology.

So what do people do who are good at engaging customers? In reality, *Engaging* a customer takes minimal time and effort. In many cases, it may only take a minute or two, but it takes a lot more than, "How can I help you?" or, "Can I take your order, please?"

During my early years of college, I worked with one of my favorite managers delivering pizzas. She was full of customer service mantras. She often reminded me of the phrase, "You only get one chance to make a great first impression." Then she added her own thoughts to the quote and would shout, "SO DON'T RUIN IT!"

Whether or not a customer service transaction is successful, can be a direct result of the first several seconds of the interaction. Think about going to a restaurant. If you enter and are seated right away, you feel like things are going well. However, if you have to wait for a hostess to seat you, followed by a long wait for your server to take your order, things are well on their way to an overall negative experience for you as a consumer. Even if the rest of the visit goes well, you are already cautious based on the start of the visit.

Engaging the guest involves acknowledging them, then talking to them on a personal level. Talk to them for more than the purpose of getting as much money from them as possible. This is the best opportunity to learn their name. Learn it and use it! People like hearing the sound of their own name and there is a "special" feeling that comes from being known by name at the places you like to go.

Just like on *Cheers*, "you want to go where everybody knows your name, and they're always glad you came."[3] Dale Carnegie cautions, "Remember that a person's name is to that person the sweetest and most important sound in any language."[4] Remember their name. This is not a one-time thing. If you are doing your job and *Delivering* great service, you will be seeing them again.

Also, remember that the goal of *engaging* your customer is to eventually *Discover* what their needs are. The authors of *Raving Fans* suggest that employees should be engaging the customer in casual conversation that is not involved with the transaction—i.e., the weather, local events, or sports.[5]

During my university studies, I had the opportunity to work at a golf course. This job afforded me a lot of customer interaction. The rivalry team of the university that I attended was only about thirty miles away, so it was not uncommon to see people in attire supporting either of the two teams. It was a great conversation starter. Isn't it a lot friendlier to say, "What did you think of the game?" rather than, "What can I sell you today?" or, "What do you want on that pizza?"

While visiting a cousin in a nearby city, we decided to go out to dinner with our families. I observed one of the servers, Christian, as he interacted with customers. He would ask them about their day at the local amusement park. When he came to our table, we began chatting and I found out that Christian was familiar with the hand stamp and attraction bracelets from the nearby amusement park. It was very easy for him to break the ice as he would simply ask, "How was your day at the amusement park?"

Imagine the casual conversation that can be sparked from this one question. Think about the message that is conveyed to customers, "I don't just want to take your money. I am happy that you are here today and I would be genuinely interested in hearing about your day." When I had an opportunity to speak with the manager later, commending Christian's behavior, he explained to me that customers frequently commented about Christian's friendly and attentive nature. Christian is a great example of someone who knows how to *engage* guests.

How do you ensure that the first several seconds go well when you meet a customer? You *engage* them. Remember that engaging the guest or customer is your opportunity to learn about them. *Engaging* the guest means that you ask questions, they talk, you listen. Ari Weinzwig explains that as you learn about your customer, you should be talking twenty percent of the time, and listening the other eighty percent.[6] This leads us into the next step: *Enquire*.

Enquire

Cammie called to order a pizza for her family from a prominent national restaurant chain. The person who answered quickly blurted, "Thank you for calling *Awesome Pizza*. Can you hold, please?" Click. Without even giving Cammie a chance to respond, the employee put her on hold. After waiting on hold for about five minutes, Cammie hung up. Cammie called back, was again asked if she could hold, but was again put on hold without the opportunity to respond. She explained to me later, as a kind of social experiment, she wanted to wait and see how long she would be kept on hold.

So she waited . . .

and waited . . .

and waited.

Cammie's curiosity began to get the best of her as she realized that the restaurant was only about ten minutes away. So, while still on hold, she got in her car and drove there. A few minutes later, she arrived at the restaurant. She walked in the front door and immediately observed that the establishment didn't seem busy. There was no one waiting and likewise no one was taking her order on the phone. After a few moments, an employee came to take her order at the counter. She ordered her pizza and was about to pay for it when she saw a second employee head for the phone.

She explained to me that it was almost fifteen minutes before she would have been assisted with her order on the phone. While the girl who took Cammie's money did *engage* her, she didn't really ask about anything except how she could help make Cammie's wallet a little lighter. Of this incident, Cammie said, "*She did ask* who I was on the phone with. I lied and said it was a friend. But now looking back I wish I would have said, 'I'm on hold with you waiting to order a pizza.'"[7]

The second skill associated with *Discovering* what your customer needs is to *enquire*. This is where you get down to the nitty-gritty of why they are your customer. Work to really *Discover—enquire* about what they need from your business. *Engage* them by doing more than just putting them on hold, and then *enquire* about their specific needs.

Few businesses have success in guessing what their customers want—even though they often try. Here are some questions you may want to ask:

- Is this your first time visiting our facility (or using our product)?
- How did you hear about us? What brought you in today?
- If it's not their first time, find out what brought them back. Is it the product? The service?
- Did they come in because of a coupon or special offer?
- Are they aware of your online presence (assuming you have one)?

- How many people are they expecting? How many participants need to be serviced?

I worked at a fast food restaurant through most of high school. At places like the one where I worked, the goal during lunch time is to have every car through the drive-thru in ninety seconds or less. Some people see it as an equation that looks like this:

Speed = Great Service

The reality is, speed does not equate great service. It may be one element of *Delivering* service, but should not be used as the primary means of measurement. *Engaging* and *enquiring* should take as long as necessary to take care of your customer. Interestingly, an article published by QSR Magazine showed that while Wendy's had the fastest drive-thru time, they tied with McDonald's and Burger King for the least polite employees.[8]

As previously mentioned, taking your time with each customer doesn't mean that you can ignore all the others, but rather, acknowledge their presence, and let them know you will be with them as soon as you can. Few people will mind waiting when they see how friendly you are and that you genuinely care about their needs.

Those who are great at *enquiring* know how to ask the right questions. I worked with a bowling center that was set up such that when guests entered they came to the front desk. The cashier would not only charge them for games and shoes but enter the names of bowlers on each lane as well. This added a personal touch to the transaction. It also allowed service providers to find out if any players needed bumpers, how many people were playing, and how many games they planned on playing. Knowing the number of people on each lane and the number of games they would be playing was vital to operating an efficient wait-list when the bowling center was operating at capacity.

I observed that a lot of guests had trouble with the question, "How many games do you want to play?" They would stop and think about it, then discuss it with a spouse, date, or friend. Then they would think some more. They struggle because the answer could be any number of games, depending on their time constraints.

This ties in with *engaging* your customer before *enquiring* about their needs. As you *engage* them, you may get an idea of what they will want to do. Typically, a family that has younger children will only want to play one game. On the other hand, a group of college students will almost always play two.

In working with them, we found that by changing the wording, the process could be made easier for both the guest and the employee. Our employees began asking a closed-ended question, "Would you like to play two games today?"

This way the guest only has to answer "yes" or, "no." It also helped as a suggestive sale to put the thought of two games into people's minds. Our observation was that most guests would reply with either, "No, just one game," or, "Yes, two games." It made things easier for the guest as their answer now had a limited number of possibilities rather than an infinite number.

A note of caution—your job is to build relationships and make the customer happy. If a family comes in to bowl with mom, dad, and three kids under the age of ten, they will not want, let alone be able, to bowl two games. In cases like these, service providers still asked a closed-ended question, but varied the number of games. "Did you and your family just want one game tonight?" Again, they have the yes-no option, but you are starting them off with the answer they will probably give. Don't get greedy and try to upsell two games to every single person. It will only cause more work for you later when they realize they only want one game.

What else do employees do who are good at *enquiring* about their customer's needs? They listen ... a lot. Think of what it's like when you are eavesdropping. You are hanging intently on every word, syllable, and detail.

One challenge you may face is that customers don't know what they want. And sometimes, they don't know that they don't know what they want. I had the opportunity of working in the customer service department of a training company that offered communication skills to business executives. The business model was such that our organization certified trainers to train our content where that trainer was employed.

Everything was set up to be very easy for our client trainers. The whole training was available on a platform they could install on a computer after becoming certified. One of the tools we offered was a website containing exclusive content for the client trainers while offering tips, suggestions, and training outlines. It was not uncommon for customers to contact us explaining that they needed access to this website. As we *enquired* about their needs, we would often *Discover* they already had access and were actually trying to install the trainer software (which was on a USB included with their trainer materials).

Listen to what they tell you they need, and if you need to, help them figure it out. Think about when you go to a restaurant for the first time. The server is always ready with recommendations to help you decide what you want to order.

As you *enquire* about your customers' needs, listen to what your guest is telling you, but also pay attention to what your guest *isn't* telling you. Things you might ask yourself include:

- What does their body language tell you?
- Are they with other people?
- Are they alone?
- Are they on a date?
- Are they with friends?
- Are they happy?
- Are they upset for some reason?
- Do they look puzzled and lost?
- Have you seen them before?
- Are they in a hurry?
- What does their demeanor tell you?

At a miniature golf-centered entertainment venue I managed, a gentleman came in already in a bad mood. Mike, one of the other managers, observed this gentleman's attitude, *engaged* him, and *enquired* about his needs. Mike *Discovered* that the man and his children had been to three other entertainment venues that day and for one reason or another, things fell through at each of the other locations. Once he got that off his chest, he felt better, acted nicer, and it gave us an opportunity to really impress him. Mike was happy to help, and knowing that he needed a little extra attention made it easy to make his day better. This man eventually became a "regular," returning to the facility on almost a weekly basis.

Tom Connellan explains many of the "secrets" behind the incredible service at Walt Disney World in his book, *Inside the Magic Kingdom.* "At the core, [Disney employees] are all about cast members listening to guests—as opposed to listening to themselves." He goes on to cite an important example where some executives thought certain menu items in one of the restaurants should be altered. But when front-line employees were consulted, they stated that from listening to their customers, most liked the menu just the way it was. The change never happened.[9]

Similarly, with each person you *engage* and *enquire* about their needs, you have an opportunity to learn about how they use your product and what you can do to build the relationship and make them a faithful repeat purchaser.

Once you have adequately determined your customer's needs, you'll be able to recognize if they have any questions that need to be answered, or issues that need to be resolved. Oftentimes there won't be, and after *enquiring* you can move on to the second step of customer service performance which is *Delivering* what they asked for. However, there will be times that you need to be prepared with the third skill of *Discovering*, and that is to *enlighten* them about your processes.

Enlighten

Nicholas was purchasing some sunglasses at the mall. His current pair had broken due to some carelessness on his part. He decided that with his tendency to break sunglasses, he should purchase one of the cheaper pairs from a kiosk. He found a pair that he liked, but noticed that they seemed a little flimsy. Based on Nicholas' recent experience with sunglasses, he wasn't sure that this pair was the right fit.

Nicholas asked about the return policy. The employee told him he had ten days to return the sunglasses for a refund. Nicholas then asked if he were to purchase the sunglasses and they broke, could he exchange them for a new set of the same type. The employee thought about it for a minute then replied that it would be okay to exchange them ... as long as it was within ten days. Nicholas didn't buy the sunglasses.[10]

The third skill associated with *Discovering* the needs of your customer is to *enlighten* them about any concerns. Many times this skill isn't necessary. If you have properly *engaged* and *enquired* about your customer's needs, you will know if your customer needs to be *enlightened*.

Chances are that you have a good idea of some of the common concerns of your customers. This could be a wide range of things depending on your industry.

- If you are in retail, people may want to know about your refund policy.
- In entertainment, people ask about outside food.
- In food service, people ask about special orders or gluten-free food.
- In hospitality, guests may want to know about cancellation policies.
- In airlines, people will be concerned with cancellation costs and baggage fees.
- In car maintenance and repair, we all have the same questions: What is the problem? Will it take long to fix? How much will it cost? Should I just buy a new car?

If you find that there is one thing people are always complaining about, or something that always causes issues that need to be resolved, you may need to reevaluate the way you do things. For example, Walmart has been taking returns without the need of a receipt for several years. Sabrina, an associate who worked at Toys 'R' Us, explained to me why Toys 'R' Us finally decided to get on board with that same policy. They saw that a competitor was doing it and, more importantly, customers were getting upset when they couldn't return something without a receipt.

She told me about her experience with a man who came in for a return. Sometime during the summer, his son had said he wanted a polar bear for Christmas. While the man and his wife were on a date, they dropped by the store and purchased a plush polar bear. Months passed and as Christmas neared, the same child decided that he wanted an elephant for Christmas. The parents tried to reason with the child, but the kid would not change his mind. Sabrina related her experience to me: "The man approached the Service Desk. He had a friendly smile, and was very nice. He asked if we take returns with a receipt. I explained our policy; we accepted returns with a receipt if it was within sixty days of the purchase. He looked down at the receipt in his hand for a moment, and then he looked back up at me.

"'But you take returns without a receipt, correct?' he asked.

"I explained that he was correct and reemphasized our policy to accept returns without a receipt. It wasn't until I explained it to him again that I realized the ridiculousness of our own policy. He quickly shoved the receipt into his pocket and said, 'I lost the receipt, but I would like to return this polar bear.'"[11]

Sabrina took care of the return, and as she had no customers in line, *enquired* more about the man's needs. That was when she *Discovered* the reason for his need to return the polar bear that had been purchased months earlier. They joked about how silly it was that he couldn't return something, even though he had the receipt. It was more to his benefit to not have one.

Return policies are a common area where customers need to be *enlightened*. Whether it's during the initial purchase and you're explaining the policy only if they need it, or if it's during the actual return, having a clear and understandable policy is a great way to offer customer service.

I mentioned earlier that Nicholas didn't buy the sunglasses he liked. It was because he didn't like the answer about the return policy. When he and I chatted about his experience, he said to me, "What if I had bought the sunglasses, and as I anticipated, they broke after twelve days? So then I try to return my broken sunglasses and find out that the policy doesn't allow for me to exchange them because it had been more than ten days. How much more frustrated would I be?"

Like Nicholas, most of us expect that our concerns will be addressed in the initial transaction, but that's often not what happens. That's what all customer complaints really are—the gap between what was expected and what was *Delivered*. We will discuss *Delivering* your customer's needs in the next chapter, but for now let's just say that it's best to find out what your clients are expecting up front and *enlighten* them about any potential issues.

Don't always wait for your customer to bring a problem to your attention. It is advantageous to know what concerns, problems, or issues other clients have had. Then, you can be proactive, and when you perceive that there may be a concern, you can let your current client know exactly what to expect.

Enlightening your customers about their concerns is a great way to eliminate errors because the problem is being resolved before it actually occurs. If a person has a concern or a doubt that is not resolved initially, you will have an upset customer later.

Rich Sheridan, co-founder of Menlo Innovations understands this concept. Rich describes one of the founding philosophies for his software company is to "make mistakes faster." Sheridan explains, "If we make mistakes fast and discover them early, then we have a chance to correct them while they are still small and while there is still time and budget left to make changes."[12]

In the customer service world, this means that rather than making mistakes, you are catching potential mistakes early on, and resolving them up front to create a better customer experience.

A good friend of mine, Chad, told me about a time he had some work done on the engine of his car. When he returned home from his maintenance appointment, the air conditioning didn't work. He called the mechanic and set a date to bring his car back in to get the air conditioning fixed. When he arrived, he saw a recently printed sign near the mechanic's payment desk, stating that the company was not responsible for air conditioning problems that occurred while working on vehicles. Worse yet, the mechanic wanted to charge him for the repair.

Chad left furious, and after a few days went to a different mechanic who had been referred to him by a friend. This second mechanic diagnosed the issue, then, before doing anything to the car, he talked to Chad. The mechanic gave Chad the specifics on what was wrong with the air conditioning, what needed to be done to fix it, and explained the anticipated costs.

Over ten years have gone by, and Chad still takes all of his vehicles to that same mechanic. He refers all of his friends there and plans on taking his vehicles there for as long as the mechanic is around—all because the mechanic was able to *enlighten* him about his concerns up front.[13]

DISCOVER - Revisited

Alex presses "Print" on his computer, only to see the notification he hates most. His printer is out of toner. He has an important project due at work today and he desperately needs to print it. He resolves that on his way to work he will stop by an office store that has a print shop. While it will certainly make him arrive late for work, it will ensure that his project is delivered on time.

Alex enters the store and as he approaches the print desk, he recognizes the worker who helped him print a project a couple of weeks ago. She is on the phone, but sees him, smiles, and mouths the words to him, "Give me just one minute." He smiles back, reassuring her that he doesn't mind waiting.

Engage: After hanging up the phone she asks how he is doing. They converse for a moment about the great weather they have been having.

Enquire: Then, calling him by name, she asks what kind of project he will be printing (instead of asking, "What can I do for you?"). He explains his situation and gives her the USB that has his project. She asks specifics about his work, and after he explains what he is doing with the project, she suggests he use a heavier paper and have it bound.

Enlighten: Perceiving a potential concern, she reminds him that the special paper and the binding cost extra. He responds that there is not a problem with the extra cost, and agrees with her that it will make his report more effective. She prints and binds the project with efficiency, and Alex even makes it to work on time.

Summary

The three skills associated with *Discovering* your customer's needs are to *engage*, *enquire*, and *enlighten*. Acknowledge the presence of your guests, and *engage* them in casual conversation related to topics outside of the transaction.

Enquire about your clients' individual needs from your organization. Find out what brought them in or what brought them back and what makes your business different than your competitors. Learn their names! Ask the right questions, observe non-verbal cues, and listen intently to responses.

Be prepared to *enlighten* them about common concerns they might have about your product. Or let them know up front when you perceive a potential issue. Solve the problem before it occurs.

Discovering your customer's needs by *engaging*, *enquiring*, and *enlightening* will help you to improve your customer service performance and begin building business relationships with your clients.

Review

The following are some questions that can help spark discussion on where you currently are in regard to this step, and what you can do to improve both individually and as an organization.

- What are some simple things you can discuss with your guests, not related to the transaction?
- What are questions that you will need to ask your guest to complete the transaction?
- What information do you need to know? What are the best ways to word these questions?
- How can you better listen to what your guests are telling you about their needs?
- Are there barriers that can be removed to improve communication?
- What are some common concerns your guests will have?
- How can those concerns be eliminated?
- Are you able to eliminate guest concerns with a clear and concise explanation?
- Are there policies that create common concerns for customers that should be evaluated for effectiveness in customer service?
- Are there policies that are a must (i.e. government-mandated) that you could create an easily understandable explanation for why the policy is in place and how it benefits the customer?

Exercises

1. With a learning partner, work through an entire transaction. You will act as a customer, while your learning partner acts as an employee. You, as the customer, should act as if it is your first time purchasing from the business. Think about what questions you might have, information you would like to know, and what concerns you would want to be resolved. Have fun with it, ask a lot of questions, be a little difficult, but realistic. Ask questions that first-time customers often ask.

2. After finishing the entire transaction, switch roles. Run through the scenario again, but make sure that your learning partner, who is now the customer, asks different, but still common first-time questions.

3. After you have finished this second transaction, make a list of the following:

   a. Specific ways to *engage* your customer

   b. Common needs an employee will *enquire* about

   c. How, as an employee, you can *enlighten* your customer.

4. Now go through two more transactions, each of you with an opportunity to be the customer again. This time each of you will pose as a loyal customer who purchases from your business often.

5. After these two transactions, again make a list of common ways to *engage, enquire,* and *enlighten* a loyal customer.

Happy to Help   Discover

6. Compare the two lists you have now created, one from a first-time customer and one from a loyal repeat customer. Discuss the following:

    a. What is the same about how you *engage, enquire,* and *enlighten* a new customer versus an existing one?

    b. What is different?

    c. What would be the most important thing to train a new employee about *Discovering* the needs of a customer?

7. Share what you've learned with a minimum of three coworkers.

48

Extra Credit

Visit at least one competitor. Discuss with a co-worker or manager the following information about your competitor vs. your organization.

EASY: Regarding *Discovering* the needs of your customer, what do you do at your organization that is better than your competitor?

INTERMEDIATE: Regarding *Discovering* the needs of your customer, what do you and your competitor do about the same? What can you do to differentiate your organization from theirs?

HARD: Regarding *Discovering* the needs of your customer, what does your competitor do better than your organization? What needs to happen for your organization to level the playing field, or take things a notch higher than that competitor?

Worth a Thousand Words

See if you can find what the pictures below have in common. What should these organizations be doing to improve their customer service?

Hint: Before you can Discover the needs of your customer, you need to be at your front desk or kiosk, ready and waiting to serve them.

DELIVER

Tim and his family were celebrating the college graduation of his oldest son. This included Tim, his wife, Aaron (the graduate), two siblings (a brother and a sister), two sets of grandparents, and Uncle Pete (Tim's brother)—a total of ten people. Tim decided that to commemorate the occasion, they should go out for a special dinner at Aaron's favorite restaurant. Because of the size of the group, Tim decided to make a reservation. When he called, he was greeted with a pleasant voice who politely asked him to hold. After several minutes of waiting, he decided to hang up and try again. When Tim's call was answered the second time, he was given immediate attention and was able to set up the reservation. He figured that first time was no big deal, stuff happens, people get busy.

When Tim and his group arrived, they saw that the restaurant was very busy. Tim was concerned, but was comforted by the fact that he had a reservation. After entering the restaurant, Tim mentioned to the hostess that he called ahead to reserve a table for his group. The hostess smiled, and then explained that she would have them seated in a few minutes.

Five minutes passed.

Then ten.

Then fifteen minutes had gone by.

When Tim returned to the front kiosk to inquire about his reservation, the hostess responded in a stressed voice, "Yes! Right this way." The group was finally seated, and Tim reflected on his experience. "No big deal, right?" he thought to himself, "So what if I made a reservation and still had to wait several minutes? I can see that they are really busy."

After several more minutes passed, a server finally materialized and asked for the group's drink order. Shortly after, the server returned to bring the group their drinks, and then asked what their food choices would be from the menu. Several minutes later, the server returned to deliver the entrées, everything made as it should be.

The food was delicious and Tim was enjoying the celebration so much that he was halfway through his meal before he realized his drink was empty. Tim looked around the table to see that much of the family had empty drinks as well.

Their server was just passing by at that moment and Tim was able to get his attention. He pointed to the empty glasses on the table and politely explained that everyone needed refills. The server returned promptly and refilled everyone's drink, and then asked about everyone's meal. Everyone answered in the affirmative, or that it was "fine," and the server was gone like a flash.

A short while later, Tim noticed his glass was empty again. But this time his server was nowhere in sight.

"I wanted another refill," Tim later explained to his wife. "I guess it was okay. I mean, they seemed pretty busy." But as Tim looked around he began to realize that they were not that busy. He continued waiting in hopes that his server would be along to refill his drink. Tim finally gave up and asked a wandering server about drinks. This second server assured Tim that his server would be along shortly. Several minutes passed, and again Tim had to get the attention of another server insisting that he get some drink refills. Finally, his server showed up and refilled the drinks.

Despite the way things had gone that evening, Tim was looking forward to at least enjoying a tasty dessert. He smiled with excitement as he saw his server approaching without having to be flagged down. Then, without saying a word, the server dropped the bill on the table in front of Tim and sped off in a different direction to gather the soiled dishes from another table.

"So much for dessert," Tim said to himself. He decided that he was probably better off anyway. The way things had gone tonight, he suspected it would have taken another thirty minutes for a piece of cheesecake.

When Tim looked at his bill, it didn't seem to add up quite right. As he looked again to dissect the bill, he saw that an "18% gratuity for groups of eight or more" had been automatically added. In frustration, Tim thought to himself, "It's time for Aaron to find a new favorite restaurant."[1]

Tim's story is a great example of the second step of building relationships with customer service performance:

Deliver what your customer needs

This is the step that most people think they are familiar with—but really aren't. The customer tells you what they want and you get it for them, piece of cake, right?

As can be seen from Tim's example, many businesses struggle to *Deliver* basic expectations like being seated in a timely manner, refilled drinks without asking, and offering dessert, to name a few from the restaurant industry. Failing to adequately *Deliver* according to your customer's needs is one of the fastest and easiest ways to chase them off to a competitor.

The main reason that employees neglect to *Deliver* the needs of their customer is because they are only attempting to *Deliver* what is spoken. There are three things customers want, though they never ask for them. They are:

1. *They will be given exactly what they (did or didn't) request.* Giving them exactly what they ask for is a basic part of providing your product to the consumer. However, errors are still made occasionally and customers expect these errors to be resolved. Customers expect things they will never actually say i.e., that they want their product to arrive as fast as possible, they want it to be high quality, and they want it to be ready to use immediately. Why would a customer do business with you if the product you *Deliver* is consistently slow to arrive, of poor quality, unusable, or not even what they requested?

2. *They will be treated with kindness.* Starbucks CEO Howard Schultz has said, "I think, at the end of the day, we were never in the coffee business serving people; we were in the people business serving coffee."[2] Many front line employees either aren't trained,

or forget that their goal is to satisfy their customers' needs, making those customers as happy as possible. A personal, friendly, and polite touch always creates a better experience for the customer as well as that service provider. In today's world of instant media on any device, you don't have to look far to find negativity and hatred. Effective service providers go beyond that. They stay grounded in their own reality and work to simply be nice to the people they interact with. Even if you *Deliver* a perfect product every time, do you think your customer will continue to do business with you if you are hard to deal with socially, because you are rude and have no manners?

3. *They are being helped by people who are energetic and passionate.* We have gotten so used to mediocre and below average customer service, many people would not even be jaded by an experience like the one Tim had at the restaurant. Bad customer service providers would have us think that their bad service is just the way it is and there is nothing to be done. The opposite is true. Not only can customer service be good, it can be consistently very good. Customers like doing business with people who have energy around, and for, their product. Why will your customer do business with you if you have no passion for what you are offering them?

To effectively eradicate bad customer service, employees need to understand the needs of a customer, as well as how to effectually *Deliver* those needs, spoken or unspoken. There are three specific skills associated with this step of *Delivering* what your customer needs. The first skill is to do it *exactly* as the customer asked for, and understanding what should be *Delivered* even when it isn't specifically requested (like drink refills). The next skill is to do it *elegantly*, by being polite and showing off your good manners. The final skill to *Delivering* what your customer needs is to do it *energetically*, showing genuine enthusiasm for the opportunity to do business with the customer.

Exactly

Chase had an upcoming meeting with some important executives. Planning to dress for success, he checked his favorite suit and noticed that it was soiled on one of the shoulders from when he held his daughter as she ate crackers for a snack. As the meeting was still two weeks away, he decided he had enough time to get his suit dry-cleaned.

The suit had a three-button jacket, however, when it was returned to him, the lapel crease was folded and ironed incorrectly so the suit looked like a two-button jacket. He returned the suit and asked that it be fixed. When he returned the next day to pick it up, he was again disappointed to see his three-button coat folded and ironed like a two-button suit coat. At this point, there wasn't enough time to have it fixed (again) so he ignored the issue and wore a different suit to the meeting.

A couple of months passed, and Chase came across that suit coat again. He decided that he should get it fixed. He resolved on a different tactic, and went to a different dry cleaner. He explained very specifically how the previous dry cleaner had ironed the crease incorrectly on the lapel and what it should look like. He put special emphasis on the fact that if this were done properly, this new dry cleaner would become his preferred dry cleaner. In a few days, he returned to pick up his . . . two-button style suit coat. He hasn't returned to either of the cleaners.[3]

Delivering exactly is the most common issue that you face both as recipient and provider of customer service. You will have far fewer complaints about employees who are unenergetic and lackluster than you will about a customer not getting *exactly* what they expected. There are three challenges that you face as a customer service provider. First, and easiest, is *Delivering exactly* as your customer orders. Second, and slightly more difficult, is *Delivering exactly* when they don't know what they want. Third, and most difficult, is *Delivering exactly* as they expected, but didn't specifically ask for.

The first challenge is *Delivering exactly* what was asked for. Have you received a food order that was incorrect? Have you purchased a product or subscription that was not what you anticipated? Have you been to an entertainment venue where not everything works? These are all scenarios where the customer asked for one thing, but received something else—something different from what they expected.

The solution to this challenge is to adequately *Discover* the needs of your customer. When you have a clear understanding of what your customer is asking for, you can *Deliver exactly* as they request. You can *Deliver* food *exactly* as ordered, or *Deliver* the product that best meets the customer's needs, or *Deliver* a service that functions properly.

The second challenge is to *Deliver exactly*, even when the customer doesn't really know what they want. Here is an example from the bowling center. Two nights a week they offered "Fifty-fifty" nights. It was a special that started at 9:00 p.m. and ran with cosmic bowling. Customers paid a five dollar cover charge then could rent shoes and buy games for fifty cents each.

The challenge? About half of the people who would come to bowl on these nights were regulars (people who showed up at the same night, same time, every week). The other half were new to the facility, or had not been in for a while. Customers knew they wanted to bowl, but they didn't understand the pricing in relation to how many games they could bowl.

The solution in this case is to be keen on the *Discover* step that we covered in the last chapter. In that step, you have the opportunity to *enlighten* your customer about any concerns they may have. This could include something like being able to understand the pricing strategy. If things are difficult for customers to understand, and it's not something you have the power or authority to change, look at how you can make it easier for the customer by presenting or explaining it differently.

With the "Fifty-fifty" special that confused a lot of customers, someone was smart enough to see the confusion that our guests were experiencing and came up with the following, "Six dollars for the first game and shoes; fifty-cents for each additional game." This made the price easier to understand, and customers were quicker to decide how many games they wanted to play. By the time I started working with them, this phrase was commonly used to explain pricing to customers.

Over time, I worked with some of the employees to take it one step farther and pitched, "Three games for seven dollars." (Notice how that explanation went from fourteen words to five words.) Not only is it short and sweet, but it's an upsell. Guests will also stay longer which means more money spent on food and ancillary revenue.

The new pricing explanation worked so well, the bowling center raised the price the next year to, "Three games for eight dollars." (For those not in the bowling industry, most bowling centers only increase prices by twenty-five cents each year. The fact that they could raise the price by a dollar and sustain their market indicates that they were delivering a high-quality experience for which customers were willing to pay more—all due to wanting to offer a better customer service experience).

The third challenge is *Delivering exactly* as the customer expects, though they may not ask for it specifically. I emphasize this because there is a difference between knowing what a customer wants and knowing what they want, but aren't explicitly asking for. The following table illustrates some of the things that we may purchase, along with what we expected, but didn't receive.

What You Order	What You Expected (but didn't ask for)	What You Received
Food at a restaurant	Your food to be delivered in a timely manner.	Your food arrived properly made, but took an excessive amount of time.
An online subscription	Adequate features for your personal needs at a price that fits in your budget.	A plan that turned out to be more expensive than a similar plan that would fulfill your needs.
A dry-cleaned coat	The coat returned clean and properly pressed.	A dry-cleaned coat that has been pressed and creased incorrectly.

Reese and Mike, friends and coworkers who I mentioned previously, joined me in visiting another entertainment venue to check out an attraction called the XD Theater. An XD Theater is a small movie theater with anywhere between ten and twenty seats. While a movie plays, your seat moves in tandem with the action of the movie. There are also other features like lights, fans, and three-dimensional glasses that all work in conjunction to make a multi-sensory movie experience.

After watching one five-minute movie, we decided we enjoyed it enough to do it again. When we got back in line, the six people in front of us chose their seats, but the three of us were stopped before we could ride again.

"I don't have enough seats for all of you," the attendant said. This seemed like a mystery to us because there were twelve seats in this particular model and only the other group of six ahead of us. Then the attendant explained, "These are broken," pointing to FIVE of the twelve seats. No customer should have to request a movie theater specializing in multi-sensory chairs to keep all of your seats working, it is simply expected. Perhaps not surprisingly, this venue has since gone out of business.

The solution to this challenge is to understand all that should be included when your customers ask for something. In order to really understand the needs of your customer, you should take a step back and look at entering your business or purchasing your product from their point of view. This can give you a good idea of what some of the unspoken expectations are that they may have about your product. The following are some brief exercises that may help you view things as a customer.

- If you are in the casual dining food industry, see how long it takes from start to finish—putting an order into the kitchen all the way to delivering it to the table. Would you be willing to wait that long?
- If you are in the fast food industry, compare your times for making food to your number of errors. Are you making more errors when you are making food faster?
- If you work in retail, are your shelves frequently stocked with the items that people most often purchase? Are your sales and promotions easy to understand and all sale items placed so that regular priced items are not confused with sale items?
- If you work in a call center, call in as a customer and see how long you have to wait on hold. Is it an acceptable amount of time? How well does your issue get resolved?
- If you are in entertainment, do all of your attractions function at one hundred percent efficiency during your peak periods? What are the most popular attractions that aren't being used because

they don't function? (In a video arcade I managed many years ago, we were able to double arcade game revenue just by making sure all the games were working all the time.)

- No matter what industry you are in, how ready are you to *engage* your customers? In a call center, how many times does the phone ring before it is answered? In face-to-face interactions, is there always someone available at the front desk or kiosk to help a customer immediately upon entering your business?

Now that we've discussed how you can recognize some of the basic expectations of your customers, let's take a look at someone who knows how to *Deliver exactly* what is expected, whether it is spoken or not.

I mentioned before that Applebee's has been one of my favorite restaurants. I love going there because of the service which we always receive. As I mentioned, Reese and I immediately noticed that Reno, our server, stood out from his peers in how he *Delivered* service.

Reno has an uncanny ability to keep your drink full. If you look away for only a few seconds, a full cup will have magically appeared when you look back at your drink. Reno is a great example because you never have to say, "I would like a Coke . . . and keep it full!"

Does he *Deliver exactly*?

Yes.

Does he fulfill my unspoken expectation that this drink should stay full the whole time I'm there?

Yes.

Reno: 2, Bad Service: 0.

Being a pro at *Delivering exactly* what your customer needs, what they need but don't know how to order, and what they need but don't say requires you to analyze every detail of your *Delivery* process. Imagineer John Hench had this to say about Disney's success: "What's our success formula? It's attention to infinite detail, the little things, the little, minor, picky points that others just don't want to take the time, money, or effort to do."[4]

Once you have analyzed each of the small details, and every minute piece of your service puzzle so that you can *Deliver exactly* every time, you are ready to make your good service better by *Delivering elegantly*.

Elegantly

The following story was shared with me from one of my work associates, Brett:

My family recently purchased a pizza from a local pizza franchise. We ordered a large pizza and paid for it over the phone. We then left to run some errands, leaving a babysitter at home with our kids. To our dismay, we discovered a medium-sized pizza when we arrived home. In my frustration, I called the business and asked for the manager. The manager explained that they were short on dough and had to make a medium-sized pizza. To correct the problem, the manager said I would have a credit for a large pizza. I asked how I would be able to redeem my credit for the large pizza and the manager said all I would have to do is come in and say my name. I would be on the credit list and I would be able to receive my large pizza.

Sometime later, my wife and I remembered that we had a credit for a large pizza at the local store. I got into my car and drove over to the pizza place, walked inside and said, "My name is Brett and I have a credit here for a large pizza."

The man behind the counter said, "No credit."

"What?" I thought to myself. I explained to him what had happened earlier regarding the mishap of the medium and the large pizza. He then explained to me that the manager said that, "They will no longer give credits to anyone."

I explained to him that I was guaranteed my large pizza and all I had to do was come in and give my name, and I would be on the list of people who had a credit for a free pizza. He didn't say anything, he just stared at me. So, I asked to talk to the manager. He said that HE was the manager and that the franchise had been taken over by new management shortly after my mishap.

I explained to him that this is still the same store with the same name on the store. He once again said that no credit would be given. I then asked to talk to the manager above him at which point he said that he was actually the franchise store owner.

I had had enough of this clown and said goodbye to him. Why hadn't he just explained to me that he was the owner in the first place? Rather than letting me pull my hair out trying to get my problem solved.[5]

There are a variety of customer service issues Brett experienced including *intentionally* being given the wrong size pizza and later not being able to receive what he paid for. We'll talk more about customer retention and how to fix errors in a later chapter. What I would like to focus on in this story is how rude the manager/owner was to Brett. He definitely was not happy to help. What he lacked, in a word, was *elegance*.

Delivering elegantly means that you need to be a genuinely nice person and practice good manners. Be polite and use kind words. Talk to people in a nice way. Do nice things for them, anticipate their needs, and use your manners (yes, I said that twice). Say *please*, *thank you*, and, *you're welcome*. When a customer says, "Thank you," be sure and respond! Obviously, my go to phrase is "Happy to help!" But I some-times say "Thank *you*." But you can say anything like, "You're welcome," or, "Please let me know if there is anything else I can do for you." It is no accident that when you eat at Chick-Fil-A you will always hear, "My pleasure." It's not like one employee said it and it caught on. It is a delib-erately trained habit by people who understand great customer service performance for building relationships.

Please, please, please don't use "common" language or slang. Phrases like "No problem," or, "Anytime," should be avoided. Your cus-tomer may not notice or care if when they say, "Thank you", you say, "No problem," but they will always notice when you say, "You're welcome."

I mentioned before that one of the issues with fast food is that you are sacrificing good service for fast service times. I have seen cases where employees and even managers became disgruntled with custom-ers who take too long to order. Really, the customer should be allowed to take as long as they need to order, and the staff should be polite throughout the entire transaction.

I was especially impressed with a recent transaction I had at Taco Bell. When I pulled up to the drive-thru speaker, I was greeted with a friendly, "Hi, how are you doing today?" I was a little shocked at first; I didn't even know what to say.

When I worked at Wendy's in high school, one of the cashiers who had to take orders through the drive-thru would just say, "What can I get for you?" as fast as possible, when cars arrived at the speaker. In his mind, it took too long to say, "Thank you for choosing Wendy's" or, "Hello. What can I make for you today?" In his defense, the idea that those phrases took too long to say was supported by management.

So, I was at the speaker at Taco Bell, and after getting over my shock, finally responded, "I'm doing well. How are you doing?" Amazingly, the voice at the other end of the speaker said, "It's been a good day. I can't complain. The weather has been nice lately, and I'm really enjoying the warmer temperatures." In case you've forgotten, this is over the speaker at a Taco Bell, during lunch hour!

We ended our small talk and he politely, in a non-rushed voice asked, "What can I make for you today?" He took my order, and it was made to perfection. The most joyful part of the experience was the polite, friendly, and dare I say, *elegant*, attitude of the cashier.

In subsequent visits to other locations, I noticed that it was happening there as well. I asked one of the cashiers how long their transactions were supposed to be. She told me two minutes. That's thirty seconds longer than Wendy's. Imagine how valuable thirty extra seconds would be to *Discover* your customer's needs and *Deliver* them *elegantly*.

Delivering elegantly is just one of many ways that you can build strong bonds with your customers. According to Janelle Barlow and Dianna Maul, only fourteen percent of customers who switch providers do it because they are unhappy with the quality of the product—most make the move because they were dissatisfied with the service they'd received."[6]

Understanding that you need to *Deliver exactly* as your customer requested while *Delivering elegantly*, you must now *Deliver energetically*. A warning—the lack of this third skill can be detrimental to your business.

Energetically

At the bowling center one particular evening, I was chatting with customers at each table, and trying to ensure that all of the guests were having a great time. As I came from the pool hall toward the front desk, a woman bowling on the first lane asked for my attention.

She asked if the manager was present. I explained that I was the manager on shift that evening and asked what I could do to help her. She told me that the employee who set them up on their lane looked very grumpy and unhappy. They politely suggested that I should not employ front line staff who were "incapable of smiling" and providing the necessary guest service. (These were her exact words. They still ring through my ears.). She and her party were clearly unhappy with the service they were given.

Hoping I could ensure that these guests would leave happy, I asked what I could do to compensate for the poor service they'd received. The woman replied that she was not interested. As a last attempt, I offered some free passes to them for their next visit. The woman then replied, "Thank you for the offer, but we do not need the passes. We will not be coming back." In short, they were given such "unbelievable" guest service that they decided to not return, even given the opportunity to do so free of charge.

The benefit of this experience was that she was willing to talk to me. Research indicates that only four percent of customers bother to complain. For every complaint you hear, twenty-four others go uncommunicated to the company, but not to other potential customers.[7] As we will discuss in a later chapter, a complaint is a gift, and customers who complain are some of the best customers you have. Although this customer was unhappy with her experience, at least she let me know why. And she let me know, specifically, that a lack of energy was the reason for them deciding to do business elsewhere.

Being energetic can include a whole array of emotions and attitudes like being happy, friendly, enthusiastic, genuine, pleasant and all around enjoying your work. Along with being polite to your customers, guests should be able to sense your happiness and overall enthusiasm for working with people. They can tell when you are happy to help. Keep in mind that this means being energetic even when you are not really feeling energetic. It doesn't matter if you are having relationship problems, money problems, or you don't like your coworkers. These are not the problems of your customer, and frankly, most of them don't really care about your personal problems, they just want good service.

Ari Weinzwig offers a prime example: "When you go to the theater to see a play, do you really care if the lead actor is in a good mood? Do you care if the actor and actress are mad at each other? Are you concerned about whether or not the lead actress is bored with her role? I'm not. I just want to see a good show. I paid my admission fee, and I want to see good theatre."[8]

Another great example comes from the book *The Experience Economy*. The authors discuss how work should be seen as a stage, and every employee, an actor. Think about Disney and how cast members can be onstage or backstage. When they are onstage, they remain in character, regardless of what emotions or personal issues they may be facing. It's important to understand that we are talking about customer service *performance*.[9]

Several years ago, I had an opportunity to attend a seminar with Frank Price. Frank Price operates the Birthday University, a consulting practice that teaches entertainment facilities and other businesses how to *Deliver* memorable birthday party experiences. He spoke about how it isn't just about creating fun for the birthday party; it's about creating fun for everyone.

Speaking to managers, Price specifically stated, "You have to make it fun. If you are not having fun, then your employees won't be having fun. And if your employees aren't having fun, then your customers definitely aren't having fun. And if they aren't having fun, why are they there?"[10]

While part of the problem may be the attitude of employees, keep in mind that managers set the tone. If employees are not *Delivering energetically*, then look first to management's energy levels. If management is *energetic* and front line employees are not, there is likely some training that needs to be done. If the employee has been trained, and still won't do it, I suggest corrective action from management.

Am I suggesting that you terminate an employee because they will not smile or be energetic? Yes, I am. At the bowling center, our average customer group size was four people, spending an average of six dollars per person or twenty four dollars per group. Our average customer came to the bowling center four or more times per year. That's almost a hundred dollars that I lost because of a single group I knew would not be returning. Multiply that by the other twenty four people who didn't speak up and this employee is potentially costing me $2,400 in business—every time she works.

Yes, I will throw myself under the bus regarding the employee who was "incapable of smiling." I knew that she didn't always smile. I knew that she had a tendency to seem somewhat cold or lacked a desire to interact with customers. You know what I did about it? Nothing. I was still young in my customer service management career. I incorrectly assumed that my bursting ball of energy was enough to compensate for the lack of hers, and I was wrong. In addition, I knew less at that time about training employees and how to have a conversation about changing an attitude.

Additionally, I didn't have the authority to terminate anyone, and it would have been difficult to convince upper management that someone should be let go from the business because she didn't smile.

The expectation needs to be set up front, so when it is not met, it can be easily addressed.

In short, management needs to set an expectation of *Delivering energetically* when new employees are hired. If employees are not *Delivering energetically*, give them the benefit of the doubt and assume it is a skill issue, not a motivation issue. If they have been trained and still refuse to do what is expected, corrective action, including termination should be taken. It may seem harsh, but if employees can't *Deliver energetically* then they may not be a great fit for your business . . . and they are costing you thousands of dollars.

Following are a few tactics that will help you *Deliver energetically*:

- Make a game out of work. Have fun with it. Like Mary Poppins said, "In every job that must be done, there is an element of fun. Find the fun and, *SNAP* the job's a game."[11]
- Find a song that you enjoy that really energizes you and puts you in a good mood. Listen to it before you start work.
- Watch funny cat videos on YouTube before you go to work.
- Find appropriate ways that you can joke and have fun with customers. When you're having a great time, everyone else will too. Energy is contagious.
- You've heard the phrase, "Fake it till you make it." While I think it catches the essence of *Deliver energetically*, I prefer the quote, "Smile till you mean it!"

I was recently speaking with Brandon, a former coworker of mine. Our conversation turned toward property and home ownership. He shared that he had recently had a problem with his last mortgage payment. He had paid extra money into his escrow to slightly lower his monthly bill. When the next bill arrived, the extra payment had not been credited. When he called the company to address the issue, he hit the call center jackpot.

"I called and a gentleman named Will took my call. He was nice right from the start. I could hear a hint of a southern accent, and he later mentioned that he was in Fort Worth, Texas. Boy, talk about Southern hospitality. He was so nice and helpful.

"He answered and introduced himself, and politely asked what he could do to help me. I explained the issue to him, and he paused for a moment to investigate the issue.

"He quickly discovered the problem, and then briefly and effectively explained to me the reason for the error. He also explained that there is usually a lengthy process to rectify this kind of issue, but if I didn't mind waiting, he would put me on hold and see if he could resolve the problem right now, though it might take a few minutes.

"I was on hold for probably four minutes, listening to classical music. When Will returned, he apologized for the wait and joked that he knew it wasn't the most appealing music to listen to. He then explained that he was able to get approval and have the issue immediately rectified. He gave me my new total for the monthly payment. He was so happy and enthusiastic. It was clear that he really enjoys what he does."[12]

Hopefully, Will's manager understands what a great asset Will is to that company. Brandon only spoke with Will, so he doesn't know if everyone is as *energetic*. But if they are, this call center really has it figured out. Did you notice how Will even knew what the wait-music was like? Is it possible that he has called in to the contact center to see what the experience is like? Based on what I've heard about this stellar service provider, it wouldn't surprise me one bit.

DELIVER – Revisited

Tim and his family are celebrating the college graduation of his oldest son, Aaron. The celebration party includes ten people in all. Tim decides that to commemorate the occasion, they should go out to dinner at Aaron's favorite restaurant. Because of the large group, Tim decides to call and make a reservation. The phone is answered after one ring, and his name and group size are taken immediately.

Deliver exactly: When Tim arrives, he explains that he has a reservation. Although the place is very busy, his group is seated in less than five minutes.

Deliver elegantly: After being seated, less than a minute passes before Tim's server arrives to take the group's drink order. The server is kind, polite, and sincere. He returns promptly with drinks and asks for their meal orders.

Deliver energetically: Although the business continues to remain busy, Tim's server always has a smile and a joke when he is at the group's table.

Deliver exactly: As anticipated, the server keeps the drinks of all ten people full throughout the entire meal.

Deliver exactly: As Tim is finishing his main course, the server shows them the dessert menu and asks for their dessert preference. The group is again promptly served.

Deliver elegantly: Tim receives his bill and leaves a generous tip for his server. As he is leaving, the server (who has not yet bussed the table, or seen his gratuity) politely and sincerely thanks Tim by name for choosing his restaurant and allowing him the joy of being their server.

Summary

The three skills associated with *Delivering* your customer needs are to *Deliver exactly*, *elegantly*, and *energetically*. *Deliver exactly* by getting the things that your customer asked for specifically, as well as things that come as an expectation with your business.

Deliver elegantly by being a genuinely nice person that practices good manners. Be polite and use words like *please*, *thank you*, and *you're welcome*. Do nice things for them, anticipate their needs, and smile the whole time.

Deliver energetically with a full array of positive emotions and attitudes like being happy, friendly, enthusiastic, and all around enjoying your work. Customers should be able to feel the happiness permeating from you. This means being *energetic* even when you are not really feeling that *energetic*. You are a performer. Any time you are helping a customer, you are onstage and expected to be in character, regardless of what emotions or personal issues you may be facing. Smile until you mean it.

Delivering your customers' needs *exactly*, *elegantly*, and *energetically* will help you offer better customer service performance as you work to build relationships.

Review

Here are some additional discussion questions about how you are *Delivering* your customer's needs.

- How well does your business do at *Delivering exactly* what your guest needs?
- What areas need improvement?
- What are the unspoken expectations of your work?
- Why are these unspoken expectations important to your customers?
- Is your team of employees polite?
- Do they say *please*, *thank you*, and *you're welcome*?
- Where are the optimal opportunities to improve in *Delivering elegantly*?
- Who is your most *elegant* or most polite employee?
- What do they do differently from everyone else that others can learn?
- Does your team *Deliver* your product *energetically*?
- Who is the most *energetic* employee?
- What do they do differently from everyone else?
- How can energy and enthusiasm be increased in the work place?
- What can you do personally to get energized prior to going to work?

Exercises

1. With a learning partner, work through an entire transaction. You will act as a customer, while your learning partner acts as an employee. You, as the customer, should act as if it is your first time purchasing from the business. Consider what expectations you have and how they should be *Delivered*. Allow your learning partner as the employee to first *Discover* your needs and then *Deliver* them. Have fun with it; be a little difficult, but realistic. Verify your needs are *Delivered exactly, elegantly,* and *energetically*.

2. After finishing the entire transaction, switch roles. Run through the scenario again, but make sure that your learning partner, who is now the customer, asks for different, but still common first-time requests. *Deliver* their needs.

3. After you have finished this second transaction, make a list of the following:

   a. Common expectations that your customer has and how their request can be *Delivered exactly*.

   b. Prime opportunities to be *elegant* while showing respect and gratitude.

   c. Specific moments that you can *Deliver energetically* and what improvements can be made.

4. Now go through two more transactions, each of you with an opportunity to be the customer again. This time each of you will pose as a loyal customer who purchases from your business often.

5. After these two transactions, again make a list of common ways to *Deliver exactly, elegantly,* and *energetically* for a loyal customer.

6. Compare the two lists you have now created, one from a first-time customer and one from a loyal repeat customer. Discuss the following:

   a. What is the same about how you *Deliver exactly, elegantly,* and *energetically* for a new customer versus an existing one?

   b. What is different?

   c. What would be the most important thing to train a new employee about *Delivering* the needs of a customer?

7. Share what you've learned with a minimum of three coworkers.

Extra Credit

Visit at least one competitor. Discuss with a co-worker or manager the following information about your competitor vs. your organization.

EASY: Regarding *Delivering* the needs of your customer, what do you do at your organization better than your competitor?

INTERMEDIATE: Regarding *Delivering* the needs of your customer, what do you and your competitor do about the same? What can you do to differentiate your organization from theirs?

HARD: Regarding *Delivering* the needs of your customer, what does your competitor do better than your organization? What needs to happen for your organization to level the playing field, or take things a notch higher than that competitor?

Worth a Thousand Words

What do the following pictures have in common? What should these organizations be doing to improve their customer service?

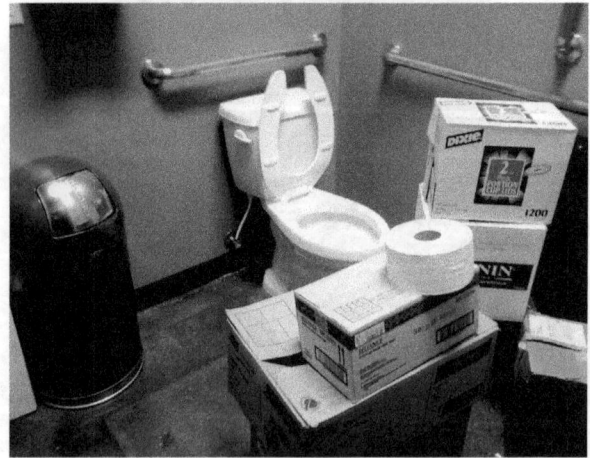

Hint: They each miss the mark on Delivering something that should be expected. The first two pictures are of the same venue but on different visits. The organization is no longer in business.

DO MORE

Jackie's son, Zack will soon be celebrating a birthday. She wants to make sure he has an extra special birthday experience. Knowing that Zack loves to bowl, Jackie decides to call the local entertainment venue. It offers a nice restaurant, a game room, and bowling lanes. Jackie also knows that at certain times they offer black-light bowling, with lots of wild lights, and good music. She knows that this is when Zack will want to have his party.

Jackie calls to make a reservation. The person who takes her reservation obtains all of the details for when Jackie's party. She becomes disappointed when she finds out that they don't offer parties during the black-light "Cosmic Bowling," but thinking it will still be fun, she books the party. The day of the party arrives and Jackie gets everyone together: her husband, her son Zack, and several of Zack's friends.

When Jackie arrives at the venue, she mentions to the employee at the front desk that she has a party booked. The employee signals to a young man who walks over, casually greets the group, and then asks for their shoe sizes. After shoes are handed out, the young man walks Jackie to her bowling lanes. He explains that his name is Mike and that he will be taking care of the party. Mike leaves the group with two sheets of paper: one with a place to list the names of the bowlers, the other is a menu that can be filled out for food orders.

Mike returns shortly to collect both sheets of paper, and in a couple of minutes Jackie and her entire group are bowling and having a good time. A short time later, food and drinks are delivered. Her group finishes eating, and eventually finishes bowling. Mike brings everyone play cards to use in the game room. After everyone uses the credits on their play cards, they return to their tables to collect their belongings.

Emily, who helped Jackie at the front desk when they arrived, delivers a party bill and mentions that she can pay at the front desk. At the front desk Jackie waits patiently in line to pay. When her bill is paid, her group leaves, discussing the scores of the game.

As Jackie listens in on the conversations, she notices that no one is really saying what a great time they had, or how amazing it was. It seems like all went well, her group was set up in a timely manner, food was delivered in the expected amount of time, all the arcade games worked, but still, it seems like something is missing.[1]

The experience that Jackie went through is an average customer service experience. There's nothing terrible about it, like the situations where employees neglect to *Discover* or *Deliver* the needs of the customer.

But there is nothing exciting, wowing, impressive, or even above-average about the experience.

Many businesses offer service like this. It's good. It's average. Maybe it's sliding toward mediocre. Unfortunately, these average experiences are not the kinds that create loyal, returning customers. To really make a great impression for your customers, and ensure that they will leave talking about how great your service is, you need to create relationships through great customer service performance. You do that by utilizing the third step:

Do more than what your customer asked for

Doing More for your customer is an opportunity to show them you are serious about being their service provider. It's how you demonstrate you really are happy to help. It shows them you care about offering more than so-so, mediocre, or average customer service. After all, this is about building relationships with your customers. *Doing More* shows that you are interested in more than just their money. It shows your customer that you value them as a person and a partner in the service you provide.

Randy White explains that there are five ways to grow any location-based business.[2] This list is in order from most effective to least effective, which is incidentally the least expensive to the most expensive way to grow your business. You read that right; the most effective is also the least expensive. The five ways to grow your business are:

1. Keep your existing customers
2. Get your customers to return to your business more often
3. Get your customers to spend more money on each visit
4. Attract new customers from within your market area
5. Attract new customers by expanding your market area

Consider your organization. How much money and time is spent on gaining new customers and expanding your market when these are the least effective means of increasing business? *Doing More* for your customer is where you have the opportunity to impress them enough to stay, invite them to visit more, and encourage them to buy more each time they do business with you. Further, as you provide better experiences, your customers will begin to give personal recommendations to colleagues, family, or business associates.

There are a variety of reasons that employees neglect to *Do More* than what their customer asked for. The most common are:

1. *They aren't empowered to Do More.* Sadly, many organizations keep a pretty tight leash on their employees. There is no room for employees to do something extra, or out of the ordinary, to exceed the expectations of their customers. Similarly, the existing processes for taking care of customers or customer resolution procedures are so rigid that employees can't resolve issues of their own accord. I once worked with an organization where all of the managers had recently read *Customer Mania*. They decided that they saw the value of changing their refund policy and giving customers their money back when it made sense. Less than one year later, the policy was in question and employees had to jump through so many hoops to get a refund for a guest, it was easier just to say they didn't offer refunds. Why would your customer do business with you if you aren't even empowered to exceed their expectations once in a while?

2. *There is no follow-up.* Most customer service organizations only think about their customers in the moment that they are doing business with them. The marketing team may be thinking about

why the customers aren't at your facility and what can be done
to get them there, but for the employees who actually interact
with the customer, the customer doesn't exist for them when
they aren't doing business. At an entertainment center I managed,
we had many regulars. We knew them by name and knew their
preferences. However, even then, we didn't think much about
that person until they were walking through the door. Why would
you expect your customer to do business with you when you only
think about them when they are standing right in front of you,
giving you money?

3. *They don't evaluate their performance, or they evaluate incorrectly.* Most,
   if not all, customer service organizations believe that the service
   they offer is satisfactory. Most of those same organizations really
   don't offer anything fantastic, but don't realize it because it has
   never been measured.

   As I mentioned at the start of this book, Forrester Research found that eighty percent of businesses believe they offer
   "superior" customers service, yet only eight percent of their customers agree.[3] Even for those organizations who do offer some
   sort of customer service specific training during their on-boarding process, they need to continually reinforce their customer
   service strategies with training follow-up.

   Measurement allows an organization to see if, and when,
   they are becoming complacent. They would never find patterns
   of complacency without measuring. Sometimes when companies
   do measure, they do it incorrectly. An organization may tout their
   outstanding service scores without realizing negative feedback
   once in a while is a good thing. If you aren't receiving any complaints, then there is a good chance people who are disappointed

with your service are just flocking to your competitor. Why would a customer do business with you if letting you know about a problem doesn't have any effect?

Like the other steps, there are three skills associated with *Doing More* for your customer. This is where you venture from the realm of good service to great customer service performance. You can *Do More* by *exceeding expectations*, giving a little *extra*, and *evaluating* your performance.

Exceed Expectations

I mentioned a server named Reno earlier who was absolutely stellar at keeping drinks full. I also mentioned that he did not write down our orders. I know some people don't like this because they are worried that the server will mess up the order. During years of eating there, and having Reno as our server, he never missed an order. Additionally, not writing orders down allowed him to maintain eye contact, show things on the menu, and keep his hands free of clutter for any unforeseen circumstance.

I also talked about how on my second visit to Applebee's with my friend Reese, we were even more impressed than our first visit. When we sat down at a table in Reno's section, he immediately brought us the very same drinks that we had ordered one week earlier.

I admit that there may be a risk like, "What if they want something different to drink?" or, "Maybe they'll only want to drink water?" Since they were non-alcoholic drinks, it is a risk worth taking. One of two things will happen. Either the customer will want the same drinks and be blown away that their drink order was remembered, or your customer will order different drinks and still be blown away that their order was remembered and be impressed by the gesture. Honestly, once you choose a drink at a certain restaurant, how often do you change it up?

Probably never.

My experience is that people are creatures of habit and typically like to stick with what they know. Therefore, there is minimal risk in Reno bringing us the drinks we ordered previously.

Reno: 3, Bad Service: 0

When we asked Reno how many orders he could take by memory, he said that he could easily do up to six and keep things straight. He was working to be able to increase that number to eight.

Another great thing about this Applebee's is the super-friendly assistant manager, John. John knows how to *celebritize* his customers. He makes everyone feel like celebrities. He always recognizes us, treats us like we are the best thing to happen to him that day, and makes sure that we have a great time. On one occasion, we observed a family leaving the restaurant. Their small child said to his mom, "We have to tell John good-bye before we leave." So they came over and said goodbye. We asked if they were old friends and John told us, "No, I just met them today."

As you can see from John and Reno's example, it doesn't have to be something huge or grandiose to impress your customers or *exceed expectations* on a regular basis. You don't have to throw in flowers, chocolates, and a giant teddy bear with every purchase. It just has to be something small that people will enjoy and remember.

As a huge James Bond fan, I was excited for the release of *Quantum of Solace* (the 22nd James Bond film released in 2009). I bought tickets for the 12:01 a.m. show for a friend and myself. After mentioning my purchase to another friend, he said he would like to go, but would be at work until 11:30 p.m., and wouldn't have time to purchase a ticket. We determined that I would purchase his ticket, and then he could meet us there, and pay me back then. When I went back to purchase a third ticket, the cashier at the theater explained that they were sold out of tickets for the 12:01 a.m. showing, but I could buy a ticket for the 12:05 a.m. showing. I explained the situation and after a couple of clicks on her computer I had my third ticket for the 12:01 a.m. show. I asked how that was possible and she said that they always save ten seats for any "emergencies." It was nice to know that my situation qualified on this occasion.

We are all used to average service, mediocre service, and experiences that are "okay." But few businesses are taking the opportunity to really capitalize on *exceeding expectations* of their customers. When you do something small, memorable, and unexpected for people you are establishing relationships with, they will want to come back AND they will bring more people with them.

One evening, while I managed the bowling center, a young man named Brian came in. He and a friend paid for an hour on a bowling lane. As their time was nearing expiration, one of the employees observed that they were almost finished with the game. However, time would expire on the lane before they were done. Seeing that no one was waiting for a lane, this employee proactively added ten minutes to their time. It was enough time for them to finish their game and they took notice. Brian thanked us, and promised to return the following week with more friends.

Brian and his "crew" as we called them, started coming in every Monday at 9:00 p.m. It started as a pair, and then became a foursome. In the following weeks there were six, then ten, then fifteen, and eventually twenty or thirty people every week . . . all because someone added a few extra minutes to their bowling lane. One minor caution for *exceeding expectations*—when you do it consistently, the better-than-expected experience becomes the expectation. So, you need to find a variety of ways to *exceed expectations* that will keep your customer family growing and coming back every week. Following are a few examples of what we did for Brian and his group:

- If Brian brought in eight or more people beyond himself, we let him bowl for free. Obviously, once he was bringing in ten or more people consistently, he rarely had to pay for bowling. I may be crazy, but I'll happily let one person bowl for free every week to ensure his ten plus followers attend consistently.

- One of Brian's friends saw that we let him bowl for free, and asked if he could bowl for free as well. I told him that if brought in ten people like Brian, he could also bowl for free. The next week, there they were with twenty people. They became regular customers AND my marketing team!

- Not many people ordered food because it was already later on in the evening. Most of them had eaten, but some of them would order drinks. We would randomly give them their drinks for free.

- As this group came in week after week, we learned their names, their bowling pseudonyms, and their shoe sizes. It was deeply satisfying to have someone approach the front desk and have their shoes waiting for them on the counter.

- Brian's group requested certain songs, so I put together a playlist for when they came in.

- We threw Brian a surprise birthday party. Each of our Monday evening employees pitched in and we bought him a toy bowling set.

- After Brian and his group had been coming consistently for about eleven months, he and I joked that we should do something special as a "one year" celebration of his being a part of our customer family. The joke became a reality and we created an offer for his anniversary. I told him that we would let anyone he brought in bowl for a discounted rate. As the group was often over thirty people, I expected to see around forty bowlers. I was shocked when **over sixty people came in** as part of Brian's crew to bowl that night! Thirty additional customers, many of which became regulars, and we didn't have to pay a single penny for advertising.

A girl named Krista also began coming in pretty frequently on Mondays. While she never brought in sixty people, she did bring in over twenty people consistently. We would put her group next to Brian's and it created a great energy between the two groups of loyal customers. Many Mondays we would have sixteen of our twenty lanes being used by these two groups, far better than any league I could have booked. I often tell people about how I had to break our "No Lane Reservation" policy to accommodate my loyal customer family. (Remember the importance of empowering your employees.) Every employee should be empowered to make choices on behalf of the organization. Every person needs to be able to *exceed the expectations* of guests without requiring management approval every time.

During my college years, I spent some time working in a national restaurant chain that sold both pizza and french fries. One evening, a customer asked me if we had cheese fries. The short answer was "no." However, we sold french fries and we had shredded cheese. Why couldn't I make cheese fries? I was in the process of telling the customer I could make the cheese fries for him when I was interrupted by my District Manager. He came over and tried everything he could to talk the customer out of ordering cheese fries and instead, to order anything else on the menu. The District Manager finally allowed me to make the customer some cheese fries, but only after the man had grown irate and was about to walk out the door. Why not just let me be empowered to take care of my customer? Empowerment is an integral part of being able to *exceed expectations*.

The authors of *Delivering Knock Your Socks Off Service* suggest that all rules and procedures are color-coded. Green Rules are ones that anyone is empowered to "break" or the things that anyone can do to help a guest. Red Rules are those that are absolutely unbreakable.[4] I would add to this Yellow Rules. These are "Proceed With Caution" rules, maybe a few things that should require a manager's approval before execution.

To really show how easy it is to do something that *exceeds expectations*, I'm including two more brief success stories. The first happened to Roscoe, an associate of mine who cut his finger at the airport. Fortunately, Roscoe had passed Sofie, an airline employee, a few moments prior and was able to find her and ask for help with his mishap. She went to two different kiosks to find a Band-Aid for Roscoe, and then completed the interaction with a hug. Regarding this situation about a stellar airport employee, Roscoe took to social media posting a picture of his bandaged finger and this post:

"I just sent the following text to Sofie's boss. 'Sofie is the best. She helped me above and beyond her required duty. I cut my finger, and she went to two different locations to find me a bandage. Wow! What an angel! On a crazy morning, I found an angel. Great employee with an amazing attitude. She was happy to help me when my minor crisis happened. A bandage and a hug. What every boy needs when he hurts his finger.' Focus on others. Truly a great way to live."[5]

The second example is from my cousin, Heather, who shares the following story.

"In 2012, I was fortunate to win a trip from my company for an award I had won. My family accompanied me to the event at a Loews resort in Florida. Loews hotels are known for their exceptional service, and it was truly remarkable. For example, when we checked in, we told the front desk agent that we would be going to dinner, but asked if someone could drop off a portable crib at our room for our baby. She said they would make that happen.

"When we returned to the room after dinner, we expected to find a pack-and-play folded up outside our room or maybe tucked inside the door. Instead, we found the portable crib fully assembled in the room, outfitted with clean sheets and a mini pillow. Even the covers were turned down for the evening. The person who left the crib had also taken the liberty of tidying up the room, leaving fresh towels, and emptying the trash. It was much more than we expected from the request, and it showed that they anticipated our every need. They knew that after a long day of travel with very young children, the last thing we wanted to do was assemble a pack-and-play, so they made it easy for us. Exceptional service!"[6]

Exceeding expectations ties back to the first principle of *Discovering* the needs of your customer. It is much easier to *exceed* their *expectations* when you know what they are expecting.

Customer Service Expert Shep Hyken explains that you don't have to do huge and grandiose things for all of your customers. Rather, he explains that as it applies to customers, "amazement is a consistently and predictably better-than-average customer experience."[7]

Extra

Rob and Laura had just finalized one of the biggest and most monumental purchases they would ever make—they purchased their first home. They were excited to take this next big step as a family, but felt some uncertainty about the process. They decided to use a realtor who had been referred to Rob by a colleague. The realtor was effective and friendly and was able to help them find the house they thought was right for them.

When it came to securing a loan, Rob and Laura spoke with one of their neighbors, Jeremy, who was a real estate attorney. Jeremy said that he would be happy to look at all of their legal documents in regards to taking out a loan and purchasing a home. Jeremy also suggested that they work with Dustin, a loan officer who Jeremy regularly recommended.

Rob checked out a couple of other sources to secure the loan and Dustin offered the best rate all around. Additionally, he discounted two hundred dollars off of his initial cost (one hundred dollars for his own services, and one hundred off of Jeremy's legal work) for working with him and Jeremy as referrals (the kind of thing that happens when you build relationships).

Overall, the process was smooth. The realtor, the attorney, and the loan officer each did a great job with their individual parts in the process. Rob and Laura assured the realtor that they would certainly use him again when the time came to look for a new home. Rob thanked his neighbor for his help, both neighborly and professionally.

Three weeks after moving into their new home, Rob and Laura received a surprise in the mail. It was a card signed by both Dustin and Jeremy, thanking Rob and Laura for the opportunity to work together. Included in the thank you note was a gift card to a very nice, elegant, and expensive restaurant; one that they usually would not eat at, simply because of the expense. Rob and Laura used the gift card a few weeks later, when they went out to dinner to celebrate their anniversary and the purchase of their new home.

While the loan officer and the real estate attorney were great to work with throughout the entire process, it was the *extra* effort after the transaction that guaranteed Rob and Laura would go back to them for their next purchase—even though it may be years away.[8]

Good organizations offer great service throughout a transaction. Better organizations make the effort to *exceed expectations* of a customer in the moment, during a transaction. The best customer service organizations go above and beyond, offering a little something *extra* even after the initial transaction.

While managing business parties and corporate events at the bowling alley, I had a woman approach me from Trapnell Orthodontics. She explained that they were planning a patient appreciation party and wanted to rent out the facility for an evening. As it turns out, there are three Dr. Trapnell's near where I live—a father and his two sons, each operating his own practice in the bordering cities. It was a lot of fun for us to provide that entertainment for them, and endearing to see an organization do something *extra* and so fun for their patients.

Years later, when my wife and I were taking the first steps into orthodontia to correct my daughter's cross-bite, we were referred to Dr. Trapnell. He recommended that my daughter should have a small bracket installed in the roof of her mouth that would space her teeth accordingly. After that process, she would need braces to straighten her teeth and move them toward the front of her mouth. Everything went well, and my daughter now has a perfect smile.

The real surprise happened during her last visit, which came as summer was approaching. The orthodontist's assistant asked how many tickets we needed for the pool party. When my wife asked for more information, the dental assistant reminded her of the Trapnell's annual patient appreciation party. This particular year, they were renting out the local water park for an evening. Tickets were not limited to patients, or patients and parents, but were expanded to include the whole family. Because my daughter got her teeth straightened, my whole family (seven of us at that time) got to enjoy playing at the waterpark—something we never would have paid for all of us to do.

Doing something *extra* and rewarding your customers for doing business with you is a great way to ensure that they will want to come back. Keep in mind that rewarding your customers with something *extra* is not the same things as having a rewards program. Rewards programs are created to reward the customer with something small after making several purchases with a company.

Rewarding your customers with something *extra* outside of a rewards program is one of the best ways to show your customers how much you really care and to give them something that really rewards. It's something nice, unexpected, and appreciated. Additionally, doing something *extra* is not limited solely to rewarding your customers. You may just follow-up to ensure the happiness of your customer. Let me briefly offer two personal examples.

The first is from Applebee's. When Reno stopped working at that store, we started going less and less until we had not been for several weeks. John, the assistant manager I mentioned earlier, connected with me on Facebook just to see if everything was okay. He didn't seem to worry about me coming back to the restaurant (he probably did, but it wasn't obvious), but was more concerned about my personal well-being.

The second experience occurred when we took my son to a

dentist. It was not the most pleasant procedure. He had baby teeth with roots that were not dissolving, but the permanent teeth were coming in. So he to have the procedure that every child fears . . . having teeth pulled. He returned from the dentist in a pretty sour mood but after a couple of days was back to normal. When his birthday arrived a few months later, we received a card from the dentist's office wishing him a happy birthday.

Incidentally, the same son needed hernia surgery a couple of years later. Similarly, we received a card in the mail signed by each doctor, nurse, and caretaker who had come into contact with my son during his procedure.

T. Scott Gross shares an experience he had regarding something *extra*. He relates a speaking engagement he had in Cincinnati. Gross's favorite restaurant in the city, Skyline, specializes in chili. He mentioned to both the group he was speaking to, as well as the folks at the Marriott where he was staying, that he was a big fan of Skyline. After returning from an audio check, Mr. Gross and his wife found a gift wrapped package in their room containing two cans of Skyline chili, two Skyline mugs, and a gift certificate for the restaurant.[9]

In the same way that many of these organizations were able to do something *extra* after the initial transaction, you should look for how you can build similar post-transaction touchpoints into your process, and create an excellent after experience for your customer. The best way to determine various options of *Doing More* for your customer by *exceeding expectations* and rewarding them with something *extra*, is to continually *evaluate* your performance.

Evaluate

Tyson had worked for Schwan's Home Delivery for quite a while. He felt that he was a pretty successful route driver and salesman when it came to selling frozen food. It was very frustrating for him when his manager, Sean, said he was coming for a ride-along. Sean had been the top salesman/route driver in his district before he moved into leadership and began managing his own depot in another state. He had a fantastic grasp of best practices for not only selling, but offering great service to each of his customers.

When they arrived at the first house on the route, Tyson brought the pre-ordered products to the door, and politely asked the woman, "Is there anything else I can get for you?" To which her reply was, "No, I'm fine. Thanks."

Sean took a moment to *evaluate* how Tyson had done and expressed that while he was very friendly, and *Delivered* the order *exactly* as requested, it was a weak attempt at upselling. Sean pulled out his tri-fold, a promotional menu that folds in thirds to easily fit in a back pocket, and asked Tyson why he hadn't used it. Tyson explained, "Oh, those are just specials that Corporate pushes on us. I do just fine without it. Besides, none of my customers want any of those products anyway."

At the next house, Tyson spoke with a man at the front door. The man was clearly a devoted customer as he spouted off order numbers, rather than product names, making it faster and easier for Tyson to enter them into his hand-held computer. When the man paused, and before Tyson could respond, Sean made his move. He quickly pulled out the tri-fold, showed it to the man, and explained that they had a special that day on a product that the man's wife was sure to love. Without hesitation, the man added it to his order.[10]

The final skill in the principle of *Do More* is to *evaluate* your performance whenever possible. Many times you may deal with one guest right after another and there is no time to stop and analyze each performance. But as opportunities allow, take time to think about how you did. As in the example above, it often helps to have someone else *evaluate* your performance, as there may be nuances that you are not noticing.

Ask yourself some basic questions:

- What did I do well?
- What could be done better next time to make the service more exceptional?
- Are customers walking away from me just okay, or fine? Are they satisfied? Or are they really happy to be doing business with me?
- Am I motivated to offer great service to each customer? Why or why not?
- Are there any skills I may be lacking in order to offer a better experience for each guest?
- Is offering great service expected and respected? Will my coworkers and teammates celebrate customer service successes with me?
- Are there aspects of my environment that can make things more efficient when it comes to *Delivering* great service? For example, when you go to the movie theater chain Cinemark to buy tickets, the employee inside the booth has a speaker and a microphone. It makes it easier to hear each other rather than talking through a shotgun blast of holes in the glass present at other movie theater chains.
- Are there aspects of your system(s) that can make things more efficient for you? Like the example of offering three games for eight dollars instead of an excessive explanation of cover charges and games and shoes and so on.

Another reason to *evaluate* is not just to improve your own performance, but to improve the performance of other individuals and the team as a whole. Positive service experiences help to uplift and inspire others. It helps them to recognize and say, "I can do that." It also helps to create an overall culture of service performance and relationship building. Relating negative experiences in a positive way (I mean sharing them, not complaining about them) can help others avoid costly mistakes.

Another aspect of *evaluating* is measuring. Measuring the quality of your customer service can help your organization avoid costly mistakes. Perhaps you have an employee who is giving substandard service. Or, maybe at specific times of the day you are not staffed appropriately. Or, maybe you have something that you offer, but your employees have a difficult time *Delivering*. Frequent *evaluation* and measurement can help you see some of those service gaps that may be less obvious.

I worked with a small business that set a goal to increase awareness, gain top of mind, and increase the number of new clients (in my mind, this is the only one of the three things they were trying to achieve that is measurable). They planned to do this by offering a promotion through Groupon for one very specific product. It seemed to work at first. The company broke Groupon's record in the region. Front-line employees noted that there were hundreds of new customers that they had never seen before. But then something interesting happened. As the expiration date to use the promotion passed, the new people stopped coming in to the business. Unfortunately, no measurement was taken so there was no real opportunity to verify whether or not the promotion was really successful.

When I was asked to help them, we agreed that we would set a standard by which to measure the success of any promotion. We examined the same product as before. Demographic and purchasing research showed that there was one day in the week that sales of that product could exceed the product sales of all other days combined. The best sales person (a higher paid employee) was assigned to work that day specifically, and given the task of pushing that product.

After only six months, sales had increased by almost fifty percent. The extra sales required the inclusion of an additional worker. After all, we want to offer the best customer service possible. Specifically, the extra worker would function as a point person who could ensure the proper ordering and fulfillment of the product once the sale was made.

After one year, sales had increased by one-hundred seventeen percent—more than double the initial sales! While additional expense was incurred on a more expensive salesperson and an additional fulfillment employee, the growth that resulted from the campaign was enough to mitigate these costs. Every dollar spent on marketing the product (additional labor) brought over five dollars in sales.

Evaluation and measurement are keys to success. Only through measurement will your organization know if it is being successful. There are obvious areas to measure like sales, headcount, and budget but let's look at some of the less obvious areas.

- Does your organization measure employee effectiveness and engagement?
- Does each employee understand how their job contributes to the overall success of the organization?
- Are they working on the projects that matter and make a difference?
- Does your organization measure customer satisfaction? Imagine if you discovered that when customer satisfaction went up, sales increased as well. Wouldn't you do everything possible to increase

customer satisfaction? Then again, how would you ever know unless you are measuring?

One more thought on *evaluation* and measurement—the results will not always be positive. The very best organizations are not the best because they are perfect. They are the best because they have made mistakes, and learned from them along the way. The truth is that most people who take surveys are doing so to get the reward. They want to get through the survey as quickly as possible, which usually means giving high marks throughout the survey without paying any attention to the actual questions.

Receiving negative feedback once in a while says that people like you, they trust you, and they want to give you another chance. If you aren't receiving any complaints, then there is a good chance your customers are choosing to do business with your competitors.

About seventeen percent of customers will change providers after only one instance of poor customer service that is not resolved to their standard. This number increases to nearly fifty-eight percent after a second instance of poor customer service.[11] If all of your customer service surveys are positive and you rarely receive negative feedback, though it may seem counterintuitive, there is a good chance your customer service performance needs improvement.

One of my favorite things about *evaluating* performances is that you will begin to see "bits" that work well for you in your position. These can be used over and over again with each guest to simplify the transaction or to create a humorous moment. The authors of *The Experience Economy* state that, "Every performer, no matter what the circumstances, should be prepared with practiced bits to seize the spontaneous opportunities that arise in the course of doing business."[12]

Having bits ready to be humorous and entertaining, or just having prepared responses for often asked questions are both important. However, neither bits nor common answers can be adequately prepared if you aren't taking time to regularly *evaluate* your customer service performance.

DO MORE - Revisited

Jackie's son, Zack, will soon be celebrating a birthday. She wants to make sure he has an extra special birthday experience. Knowing that Zack loves to bowl, Jackie decides to call the local entertainment venue. She knows that at certain times they offer black-light bowling, with lots of wild lights, and good music. She knows that this is when Zack will want to have his party. Jackie calls to make a reservation:

Engage: The person who takes her reservation is nice and friendly.

Enquire: The employee obtains all of the details for when Jackie wants to schedule the party. Jackie becomes a little disappointed when she finds out that they don't offer parties during "Cosmic Bowling."

Enlighten: The girl taking the reservation informs Jackie that she could start the party a half hour before the cosmic bowling and the party would overlap into Cosmic Bowling.

Exceed expectations: Two days before the party, Jackie receives a phone call from Mike. Mike explains that he will be hosting Zack's party, and wants to gather details about what he can do to make the party extra special.

The day of the party arrives and Jackie gets everyone together: her husband, Zack, and several of Zack's friends.

Exactly. When Jackie arrives at the venue, Mike is waiting for the group at the front desk. He gathers shoes for each person in the group and then escorts them to their lane.

Elegantly: Mike takes time to politely speak with each person in the group about how the party will play out. He also gets their names and determines who will bowl on each lane.

Enlighten: He speaks with them about their food options and takes notes on their order to turn into the kitchen. The group is bowling in just a few moments.

Exactly: Food and drinks are *Delivered* promptly and *exactly* as requested. Drinks are kept full.

Exceed expectations: About thirty minutes into the party, the lights go dim for the start of Cosmic Bowling. The first song to play is dedicated to Zack. During his pre-party phone call with Jackie, Mike learned that it's one of Zack's favorites. Jackie's group finishes eating, and eventually finishes bowling.

Energetically: With enthusiasm, Mike brings everyone play cards to use in the game room. He accompanies the group to the game room and helps some of the smaller children play the games. After everyone uses the credits on their play cards, they return to their table to collect their belongings. Mike interrupts them briefly to take a picture of their entire group for the party wall.

Exceed expectations: Mike takes an old bowling pin, spray paints it gold, and writes a big "#1" on it to give to Zack. Zack is ecstatic and loves the gift.

Evaluate: Emily, the manager on duty that evening, delivers a party bill to Jackie. She asks how the party went and how Mike did as their party host. Emily leaves a quick survey for Jackie to fill out and mentions that she can take care of payment at the front desk whenever she is ready. At the front desk, Jackie waits patiently in line to pay. When her bill is paid, Jackie's group leaves, discussing the scores of the game. As Jackie listens in on the conversations, she notices that everyone is talking about what a great time they had. Her son gives her a big hug and tells her how amazing it was and that it was the best birthday he has ever had.

Evaluate: After cleaning up from the party, Mike reviews the survey to see if there are areas that need improvement. Emily also offers feedback based on her conversation with Jackie.

Extra: Two days after the party, Jackie receives a card in the mail for Zack. It is from Mike, thanking them for allowing him to be a part of their special day. The group photo is included with the card.

Summary

The first skill to be applied when *Doing More* than what your guest asked for is to *exceed expectations*. *Discovering* needs and *Delivering* them to your guest accordingly is good service. *Exceeding expectations* is necessary to be considered a superior service provider. Make it a memorable experience, do something special for them, personalize the interaction, and they will repay you by telling their friends and family about your business. They will be your best customer and your marketing team. Remember the first principle, *Discover*. It's much easier to *exceed expectations*, when you know what your customer is expecting.

The second skill is to do something *extra* for your customer. Do something outside of the transaction or business space to thank them or show them appreciation for choosing you as a service provider. Remember, that it doesn't need to be something big and expensive, just a simple follow-up to show your customer you care about maintaining a business relationship with them.

The final skill of *Doing More* is to *evaluate* your performance whenever possible. Ask yourself: What did I do well? What could be done better next time? What can I share with my team to prevent future service gaps? What can I share to uplift and inspire them? You *evaluate* not only to improve your own performance, but to improve the performance of other individuals on the team. It also helps to create an overall culture of service. Relate negative experiences in a positive way (sharing them, not complaining about them) to help others avoid costly mistakes.

As you *Do More* for your customers by *exceeding expectations*, offering *extras*, and *evaluating* your customer service performance, you will become a great service provider, and in the process build great relationships with your customer family.

Review

Here are some more questions to initiate discussion about how you can *Do More* for your customer.

- What are things that you are currently doing to *exceed the expectations* of your customer?
- What else can you do to *exceed expectations*?
- Are there aspects of your setting and systems that, if improved, would make it easier to *exceed expectations*?
- Are you and other employees empowered to *exceed the expectations* of your customer?
- Do you show appreciation to your customer by giving them something *extra*?
- What can you do that is cost effective to thank your customer for their business?
- Do you frequently *evaluate* your performance?
- Are there ways to *evaluate* that you are currently not using, either as an organization or individually?
- What are the areas you know you need to improve? What are the areas that you know you do well?
- Do you share stories of failure with other employees? Do you learn from these negative experiences? Do you learn what you can do better in those same circumstances from your coworkers?
- Do you share stories of success with other employees? Do you learn new ways that you can better serve customers? Do you share stories to motivate, uplift, and inspire each other?

Exercises

1. With a learning partner, work through an entire transaction. You will act as a customer, while your learning partner acts as an employee. You, as the customer, should act as if it is your first time purchasing from the business. Allow your learning partner as the employee to first *Discover* your needs and then *Deliver* them. Your learning partner should also *Do More* for you, as the customer, by *exceeding expectations*. They should explain how they can follow-up or do something *extra* for you, and then *evaluate*, personally, their service performance.

2. After finishing the entire transaction, switch roles. Run through the scenario again, but make sure that your learning partner, who is now the customer, asks for different, but still common first-time requests. *Deliver* their needs. *Do More* for your customer by *exceeding expectations* and doing something *extra*. *Evaluate* your own service performance.

3. After you have finished this second transaction, make a list of the following:

   a. Common ways to *exceed* the *expectations* of your new customer that are efficient and cost effective.

   b. Prime opportunities to do something *extra* for your customer outside of the transaction.

   c. The moments when you can take a few minutes to *evaluate* your service performance.

4. Now go through two more transactions, each of you with an opportunity to be the customer again. This time each of you will pose as a loyal customer who purchases from your business often.

5. After these two transactions, again make a list of common ways to *Do More* for a loyal customer.

6. Compare the two lists you have now created, one from a first-time customer and one from a loyal repeat customer. Discuss the following:

   a. What is the same about how you *Do More* for a new customer versus an existing one?

   b. What is different?

   c. What would be the most important thing to train a new employee about *Doing More* than what your customer asked for?

7. Share what you've learned with a minimum of three coworkers.

Extra Credit

Visit at least one competitor. Discuss with a co-worker or manager the following information about your competitor vs. your organization.

EASY: In regard to *Doing More*, what do you do at your organization that is better than your competitors?

INTERMEDIATE: In regard to *Doing More*, what do you and your competitor do about the same for your customers? What can you do to differentiate your organization from theirs?

HARD: In regard to *Doing More*, in what ways is your competitor doing better than your organization? What needs to happen for your organization to level the playing field, or take things a notch higher than that competitor for customers?

Worth a Thousand Words

These pictures are ones that I was able to capture of service providers *Doing More* for their customers.

Mike and the gold bowling pin.

I went to Taco Bell and asked for a soft taco with my order. I was pleasantly surprised to find a CRAZZY SOFT TACO!

At a Medieval times-themed work party, this carriage driver was giving rides.
My daughter mentioned how much she loves horses.
He let her sit up front with him and even hold the reins to drive the horses.

Halloween 2009 with Brian's crew. Brian is Papa Smurf, I'm the cat with sunglasses.

Halloween 2010 with Brian's Crew. There were more people with both of these groups, but we took the picture of everyone in costumes.

February 2011 with Brian's crew celebrating a birthday for Aja (pronounced Asia), sitting to the left of the giant bowling pin. There are thirty people in this picture.

SERVICE RESOLUTION

Bryce has been asked by his company to start a new training program. He receives the parameters from the VP of his department and begins looking for the program that he believes will best suit the needs of his organization. After finding the program, he attends a course, and then receives certification to train the course in his organization.

As he prepares to train his first course, he goes online to order materials. When the materials arrive just a few days before training, he sees that they are not the materials he needs for his course so he calls the support number to get a resolution.

"Thanks for calling General Business Training Associates Incorporated. This is Jeff. How can I help you today?"

Bryce explains, "I recently went through your certification. I plan on training in a couple of days, and wanted to double check that all of my materials are ready. My materials arrived, but they don't seem to be what I ordered"

Jeff asks for Bryce's information and finds his profile on the company account management system. "I see here that you placed an order for Product X, is that correct?"

"That is correct, but I opened up the packages you shipped and it's all Product Y," Bryce replies.

"Perhaps you could double-check your order," Jeff suggests. "It says here on your account that you ordered Product X and were shipped Product X."

Exasperated, Bryce explains what he has received and Jeff verifies that it is in fact Product Y. Jeff suggests that he can manually re-enter the order and have it overnighted.

"That would be great!" Bryce exclaims.

"I'll have the invoice with the shipping charges sent to your accounting department," Jeff adds casually.

"Wait, what shipping charges?" Bryce asks.

"The charges to overnight the product," Jeff replies.

Bryce pauses for a moment to decide how to respond. "Let me see if I understand this. You guys sent me the wrong product, and now you're going to charge me to ship the right one?"

"That's our policy," Jeff explains. "I can't give approval to ship overnight for free without the proper approval."

"Well, doesn't it make sense to get that approval?" Bryce responds.

"I'll see what I can do," Jeff replies obnoxiously. "I'll send you a form that you will need to fill out. Once I get that back, I'll submit it to my manager, who can send it to the accounting department to remove the extra charge. Also, you'll need to ship back the stock of Product X that you have."

By this point, Bryce is extremely frustrated and says, "Whatever. Send me the form and the products you were supposed to ship. We can sort out the details another time." Then he hangs up the phone.[1]

This situation may sound extreme, but it is a true story that I witnessed first-hand. The first three chapters focused on how to create better customer service performance within a transaction. However, no one is perfect. People mess up. Mistakes are made. *Delivering* does not always meet the expectation that was *Discovered*. Here's what we'll be discussing in this chapter.

Discover, Deliver, and Do More for Service Resolution

When service gaps occur (a variation in what was expected and what was *Delivered*), business operators are often choosing to either ignore customer complaints, or resolve them inadequately. Those employees that are the best at their craft understand that Service Resolution is just as much a part of taking care of customers as the first three steps we discussed. Those that are the most successful also understand what data and research has proven; a five percent increase in customer retention can boost profits by twenty-five to eighty percent.[2]

An increase in customer retention leading to an increase in profit should be no big surprise. John A. Goodman found that the cost of gaining a new customer is nearly five times that of keeping an existing one.[3]

Additionally, properly creating resolution to a service gap increases customer loyalty. T. Scott Gross shares that satisfied customers are price sensitive, whereas loyal customers are emotionally sensitive. In this respect, loyal customers have to save more than twenty percent before switching service providers. Fifteen percent of customers who have a great relationship with your organization will never switch.[4]

Armed with this data and understanding of the importance of Service Resolution, why isn't everyone doing it? There are three reasons which seem to stand out as to why businesses fail to solve service gaps for their customers. They are:

1. *Lack of training.* Believe it or not, not everyone is a social savant. Even those who are can take it personally when a customer complains. When a customer voices a complaint, the immediate reaction is to become defensive. After all, that's my product, or store, or business you're talking about. In many cases, a person's job or career is their life. Others think of it like a member of their own family. It's difficult when customers say things like, "You screwed up!" The customer is most likely referring to the company, not the individual, but it's hard to see that in the heat of the moment. Imagine a flight being delayed due to weather and a customer says, "You're going to make me miss my connecting flight."

    Organizations need to train employees to understand that when a customer complains, has an issue, or presents a service gap, it should not be perceived as a personal attack on the individual helping them or toward the company; the customer simply wants their problem solved. The organizations who offer the best customer service performance don't only fix service gaps, they welcome them. Why would anyone want to do business with you if they can't approach you about a mistake?

2. *They just don't know how.* At first glance, this may appear to be the same as the first reason, but here's the difference. The first point is specific to when people complain. This points to what happens

after you've received their complaint—what will you do to fix it for them?

While most businesses preach great customer service, few have a training program in place to help a new employee understand what they can do to fix service gaps. In a retail, restaurant, or entertainment venue for example, the bulk of training is built on processes like operating a cash register or turning an order in to a cook or chef. Very little time is spent exploring the many possible service gaps, as well as what can be done to resolve common gaps. I had the opportunity to work with a small business owner who didn't offer refunds, only credit on gift cards. This was usually fine, but some customers just wanted their money back and grew increasingly frustrated at the gift card only policy. Why should your customer continue to do business with you if you can't adequately solve service gaps?

3. *They aren't empowered.* Sadly, many organizations keep a pretty tight leash on their employees. There is no room for the employees to do what they think is necessary to *exceed expectations, Deliver* something *extra,* or resolve service gaps for their customers. In many cases, the existing processes for taking care of customers or customer resolution procedures are so rigid that employees can't even resolve issues of their own accord.

I worked with an organization several years ago that (sort of) trained employees in what to do when customers complained or presented a service gap. Employees were trained to Smile, Listen, Apologize, then go get a Manager (SLAM). What it really means is—and your customers know this too—act like you care, pretend you are sorry, then go get someone who can really do something about it, because you are just a minimum wage employee who isn't allowed to do squat. This, of course, leads to an already disappointed (and now slightly more upset) customer having to repeat the whole issue all over again. This teaches customers the erroneous idea that regular employees can't solve their problems and they must always talk to a manager to get things done. Why would a customer do business with you if you are unable to easily fix their problem and create Service Resolution?

To overcome these obstacles, businesses need to train their employees with an understanding of how to react when a customer complains as well as what they can do to resolve service gaps. Furthermore, when front-line customer service employees are sufficiently trained in Service Resolution, organizations need to allow them the freedom to put solutions into action.

There are three specific skills associated with this step of creating Service Resolution. The first skill is to *Discover* what was expected by your customer and what they actually received. The next skill is to *Deliver* the needs of the customer as necessary to close the service gap. The final skill is to *Do More* for your customer, being *empowered* to fix their problem as well as offering a little something *extra* for the error.

Discover

The first issue that typically occurs when seeking Service Resolution is that the employee who is tasked with fixing the problem fails to adequately *Discover* the customer's issue. Personal feelings often get in the way when a customer complains. To the customer, you are the company. When a customer comes to you with a complaint they hope (and in many cases expect) that you will be able to fix it for them. Employees, on the other hand, take it personally. They may even feel like they are being personally attacked. In some cases, they are being personally attacked. Keep in mind that a customer who has been wronged is simply seeking resolution. They seem like they are taking it out on you because at that exact moment you are the face of the company. But in most cases it isn't personal.

A service gap occurred for my wife and I when we recently purchased new cell phones. My wife's phone immediately started having problems. Every time she went to the store, they took her phone in the back room to "fix" it. In my mind, this looks something like turning off the phone, taking out the battery, putting the battery back in, and then turning the phone back on. I've heard that it may even include checking your phone for any juicy pictures, but that's just a rumor. After three trips to the store, my wife's phone was still not fixed.

Based on what we've talked about so far, the likely reason for the repeated service gap is that the employees aren't taking time to *Discover* what the issue is with the phone to actually create resolution. I mentioned before that some employees take it personally when someone complains—these guys couldn't have cared less, which is just as bad, but on the opposite side of the spectrum. They don't really care what's wrong with the phone, or if it gets fixed, they just want to make their commission for selling the new iPhone. Okay, I'm making a lot of this up. Maybe they legitimately tried fixing it and failed three times. I find that hard to believe, but the whole process that I just went through is what your customer goes through when you aren't fixing their problem. Robert D. Dewar, a professor of Organizational Behavior at Northwestern University calls this, *The Law of Bad News.* "Stories about your service failures get juicier and worse every time they are told. You can never win a storytelling contest with a customer."5

Let's briefly cover the three steps involved with *Discovering* what your customer needs in regard to Service Resolution. There's a good chance you have some familiarity with these steps.

Engage

We will again *engage* the customer as before. If you helped them before, remember and use their name. If you were not the first person to help them, learn their name. Learn about them and how they use your product. Use casual conversation. Don't get defensive when they complain about something, even if it was *your* fault. Remember, they just want, and deserve, to have their problem fixed.

Enquire

Enquire about the situation to understand what went wrong. Why is the guest dissatisfied? What expectation wasn't met? Attentively listen and acknowledge that you heard *and* understand what their complaint is. Let them express all of their frustrations. Don't interrupt them. Don't argue with them. Don't raise your voice. If needed, ask questions to clarify the customer's concern. Remember that any concern, no matter how small it may seem, is a big deal if it matters to your guest.

Enlighten

Acknowledge that there is a service gap. *Enlighten* and educate them that you are on their team. Let them know that you are accepting responsibility for the service gap. Don't push the problem onto someone else or blame a co-worker.

"It's our kitchen guy's fault. He can't do anything right."

"It's our cashier's first day."

"The tech guy was supposed to fix this last week."

These excuses don't fly. You are making your team look bad, and you look bad speaking about them in a negative way. Besides that, the customer doesn't really care whose fault it is, they just want it fixed. So accept responsibility as if it were your fault, even if it wasn't.

Empathy (*Bonus Skill for Service Recovery*)

Be *empathetic*. Take your customer's side. See things from their perspective. Let them know you are on their team. Understand why they are upset and be upset with them. Most importantly, apologize for the error. Be sorry and mean it. Be sure to let them know what you are apologizing for. "Sorry for the inconvenience," doesn't cut it. You need to say, "I'm sorry that order was made incorrectly," or, "I'm sorry about the miscommunication as to which materials were to be shipped."

Enquire Again (*Bonus Skill for Service Recovery*)

This time you are *enquiring* about what you can do to solve your guest's challenge. What's the best way to figure out how to make things right? Ask your customer. A lot of people are scared of this approach because they are worried that a customer will take advantage of them. My experience shows that most will ask for less than what I would have given them had I been left to guess how to fix their challenge. Some people are worried about dishonest customers, but I'm with Ari Weinzig on this one. "Will some people lie to take advantage of you? Probably, but most won't. It's not worth losing the ninety-five percent of honest people just to make sure the other five percent don't get more than they should."[6]

Had my wife and I been treated with the skills listed above, my cell phone carrier would have had my complete fidelity. Sadly, after so many failed fixes, I was contemplating putting an end to my relationship with them. On a Saturday morning, I called Customer Service again, and this time I was ready to go in with my guns blazing! That was when I met Alissa. The first thing Alissa did was listen. She heard the whole story I just explained to you. Then she was kind and *empathetic*. She apologized, and took my side. She specifically said things like, "I'm sorry that phone's not working for you," and, "I would be really frustrated too if I had made so many attempts to get it fixed and it still wasn't working." My favorite was, "That's not fair that you should have to purchase a new phone when we gave you a defective one."

Alissa gave me a couple of options for what we could do. One of those options—the one I chose—was for her to ship us a new phone free of charge. It even arrived by Tuesday like she said it would. And just like that, our problem was solved.

So why did it take so long to get to such a simple resolution? I believe it is because the company does not have a clear vision of what the objective is and how that objective will be accomplished. They want to make money, but don't recognize the best way to accomplish that is by taking care of their customers and creating Service Resolution. As Alissa mentioned to me, store managers don't want to give up a phone because it messes with their inventory. This cell phone carrier is the only one I've ever used, and after eleven years as a customer, they nearly lost my business because they put inventory above their customer.

Joseph Grenny and his colleagues recently determined in a research study that each bad customer service experience can cost an organization thousands of dollars. He explains how a friend of his received poor service from an airline gate attendant and planned to never return to that airline again. Their study cites that, "A typical employee witnesses nineteen poor customer service incidents per year." He adds that,

"Those incidents together result in a seventeen percent drop in revenue annually per affected customer." He further explains that each bad customer service experience costs the company an average of $54,511 per year.[7] This means 54,511 good reasons to work hard at *Discovering* why your customer is upset, and fixing it for them.

Now that you have listened to the customer, understood what their need is or where the service gap occurred, sincerely apologized, and enquired about what you can do to create Service Resolution, you are ready for the next skill.

Deliver

Once you have found out what you can do to make things right for the customer, the next skill is to *Deliver* it. Training is the number one reason employees have trouble *Delivering* and creating Service Resolution. They are not sure what to do when a customer complains, or what they can do to fix the problem, or they aren't *empowered* to do so. Remember, when you do fix a problem, be specific about the problem you are fixing for your customer.

A few months back, Mike, Reese, and I went to a local restaurant that serves a pizza buffet. There is a large banquet room in the back which, when not being used, is open to the public. We like to sit there because we have our own seats away from the crowd, there is a soda fountain in that room, and we can watch ESPN without being disturbed by the noise or conversation of other diners.

On this particular visit, we went to our usual seating and noticed a large group of twenty or so people. They seemed to be having some sort of business lunch. This didn't bother us, so we sat at a convenient table. We observed conversations between a couple of folks in this large group and the restaurant manager. It was obvious that there was a concern on their end about us sitting in the banquet room with them. After a few moments, one of the employees turned off the televisions. Things got a little more serious for the business lunch and things got a little more awkward for us.

The manager of the restaurant arrived shortly after and explained to us that this group was a walk-in, had given him no notice, and had requested the TVs to be turned off. Like a good manager, he also asked about our experience. Reese commented that the credit card machine took a long time to process his credit card. The manager acknowledged and apologized, then returned to his other duties.

As the business meeting continued, we decided to move into the main dining area so we could watch Sports Center. After a few minutes of conversation, this same manager appeared and mentioned that he would have a special treat for us when we were done eating. At the end of our meal (if there is a definitive end to a buffet), he brought us a delicious cookie and ice cream dessert which we appreciated.

He said something like, "Sorry again about the inconvenience." While the gesture was appreciated, we were left to wonder, what was the inconvenience for which he was apologizing? Was he apologizing for the slow credit card machine? Was he sorry that they had to turn off the TVs in the banquet room? Or was this dessert because we were inconvenienced and had to move?

So let's take a deeper dive into specific skills of *Delivering* for Service Recovery. They are to *Deliver exactly*, *Deliver elegantly*, and *Deliver energetically*.

Exactly

By now your customer has complained, and having been properly *engaged*, you understand what went wrong, and what you can do to create

Service Resolution. The customer has given you the gift of a second chance, so take care to get it right this time, *exactly* to their expectation. Take responsibility and act immediately to resolve the problem.

Sometimes it makes sense to let them know exactly what you are doing to fix their problem. When I managed at the bowling center, I had a bad habit for how I reacted to a specific gap. On occasion our pinsetter machines would jam, and would not reset the bowling pins. When people would tell me about it, I would just say something like "Oh," and then run off to fix it. One of my observant coworkers brought this to my attention and we agreed that a simple, "Let me go fix that for you," was the best way to go.

Elegantly

Be polite. Remember that you are on the side of the customer. You are their advocate in resolving the issue. Don't go around the corner and complain about them, they are the reason you have a job! Earlier, I mentioned that some of the best words you can use are words like *please*, *thank you*, and *you're welcome*. *Thank You* will be one of your most powerful phrases you can use when you are trying to fix things for a customer. Remember, they gave you a gift, the opportunity of a second chance. When someone gives you a gift, you should thank them for it. This is how you let them know that you are really happy to help and serious about sustaining a business relationship.

Only four percent of customers bother to complain.[8] Of those who don't complain, many will show how they feel with economic criticism. They don't say anything, and just go to a competitor next time. So it makes sense to be appreciative that your customer is giving you another opportunity for success. Additionally, a customer bringing an issue to your attention may allow you to fix a common gap that several customers have experienced/are experiencing. You should be grateful for the few people that do speak up.

Energetically

Maintain a positive attitude. Stay happy, friendly, and energetic throughout the whole process. If you are happy and make the situation light-hearted, they will almost always follow suit. Unfortunately, some people are just having a bad day and they will take it out on you. Don't let a bad experience or an angry customer get you down. Think of it as an experience that you can learn from and offer better service in the future.

Empowerment (*Bonus Skill for Service Recovery*)

Every employee needs to be able to make things right for the customer. They shouldn't need to go through managers, or make customers retell their situation over and over again to find resolution. The first person they make contact with should always be able to fix the problem.

During my early years of college, I worked in a video store. An interesting thing that frequently occurred there is what I call "Manager Syndrome." If you have ever been disappointed with the service you received from a business (that's all of us), you have likely been a carrier of this illness. I'm not saying it's a bad thing—it's just proof that poor customer service performance has trained us to not hold businesses to a very high standard.

Here's an example. A customer comes into the store and spends a few minutes trying to decide what movie(s) to watch. As they are checking out their selected rentals, an alert pops up on their account that they owe a late fee for a movie. So I explain, "It looks like there is a late charge on here for Titanic." From this point, the responses go about fifty-fifty. Half of the people say something like, "Yeah, I brought that

back late, I'll go ahead and pay for that." The other half usually says
something like, "No, that shouldn't be on there. I remember bringing
that movie back on time," and their Manager Syndrome starts to flare.

This is a sticky situation. I either have to:

1. Argue with the customer until they agree with me (not likely),
2. Decide that the customer is always right despite the fact that the
   computer tells me the movie was four days late and just delete the
   late charge, or
3. Let them off this time, but remind them that they will have to pay
   for it next time (This doesn't really solve the problem either. It
   just ensures that they'll get mad at one of my coworkers later on).

Before I continue, there are two things you should understand
about the processes of a video store. The first is that we did really try
to give every customer the benefit of the doubt. Movie drop boxes
were checked at the end of the night after closing in case anything was
brought back last minute. Then, we checked them again first thing in the
morning when opening the store. On that opening round of check-ins,
we deleted fees for anything due the day before. That means if your
movie was due back on Friday, as long as you returned it by opening on
Saturday morning, there would be no late fee.

The second thing you need to understand about the process is
that we were actively trained and reminded that we needed to collect late
fees from customers. A movie (especially a new release) that doesn't get
returned is a movie that we can't rent; which means we're losing money.

So there I am. I have a customer in front of me who is about
to jump over the counter and punch me in the face because he doesn't

believe his movie was late, when he succumbs to, "Manager Syndrome." It sounds like this,

"I want to talk to your manager."

This is frustrating for the customer because now his time is being wasted. It's also frustrating for me because many times my manager was polite, friendly, and happy to delete their late fee. Not only does this create the feeling for customers that only managers can get anything done, but it also sets a double standard for the employee. "You work hard to collect those late fees. If anyone complains, I'll be the good guy who deletes it."

As I worked other jobs where I was more *empowered* to fix problems, I improved. When someone who was already programmed with "Manager Syndrome" would approach me and ask for a manager, I would politely ask, "Is there something I can help you with?" Some were willing to share their problem, others more resistant, but I was able to create Service Resolution almost every time.

Service Resolution is vitally important to your company as successful recovery spawns positive word of mouth and can have twenty times the impact of regular advertising.[9] Your customer-facing employ-ees are an incredible asset. *Empower* them, and stay out of the way so they can get their jobs done.

Do More

At this point, we have *Discovered* the problem, and *Delivered* Service Resolution. This is *good* customer service. However, good service is often not enough. On top of that, there is the inconvenience factor. Your customer had to take the time and effort to inform you that you *Delivered* a sub-standard product. Fixing the problem for them is really just what they deserve. Those that have the best customer service performance take it a step further by *Doing More*.

When things go wrong, you need to make it right for the customer. Business organizations often fear the expense that may go into creating Service Resolution, but their concern is misplaced. Organizations create processes and policies designed to make money, but this focus on revenue causes them to lose it. The point is that when you take care of your customer and focus on relationships, the revenue follows, not the other way around. In entertainment, it is not uncommon to see a sign like this:

NO OUTSIDE FOOD OR DRINK ALLOWED

The idea behind this policy is simple. If customers cannot bring in their own food, they have to buy yours. There is nothing essentially wrong with this policy. But there is a conflict when your company policies are both, "The Customer is Always Right" AND, "No Outside Food or Drink Allowed." When a customer walks in with food from another vendor, what do you do?

Let's take a quiz. Do you:

A. Not worry about it. They are the customer and they are always right, right?
B. Politely explain to the guest that they should remember on their next visit that no outside food or drink is allowed.
C. Ask them to put their food (like a pizza for example) in one of your boxes so that other customers won't see it and think it is okay to bring in outside food.
D. Ask them to throw it away.

E. Better yet, throw it away yourself.

F. Ask them to take it back outside. (For the service impaired, this
is the equivalent of asking them to leave, telling them you aren't
interested in their money, and really don't want a business relationship with them, all in one fell swoop.)

My past service experiences made coming up with these answers a
cinch. I have seen every one of these actions employed (except **E**, I just
threw that in for fun). I saw a District Manager do **C**, while a General
Manager I knew was keen to stick with **D** and **F**. Maybe you are wonder-
ing what I would do. Hopefully, you know me well enough by this point
to know my answer would have been **A**—just let it slide. If someone
called and asked if our establishment allowed outside food, I would
politely explain that we do not (**B**). But if they have already arrived, it's a
different story. It looks like a math equation.

The guest has outside food,

    = They do not know your policy on outside food.

    = They probably have not been there before.

    = They are a first time guest.

    = You want to make a good first impression.

    = Don't ask them to get rid of their food.

Therefore,

    The guest has outside food

        = Don't ask them to get rid of their food

Sadly, I have even seen a General Manager ask a group of customers to leave with their outside food, when it was late at night and all

of our own food service equipment was shut down. Remember, put the people before the profit. When you are more concerned about people bringing in outside food, you may make foolish choices that encourage them to not want to come back. Your preoccupation with money has forced you to lose money.

People who come in with outside food do so for one of the following reasons: they don't like your food (so they are never going to buy it anyway), you only offer one kind of food when they want something else, or they simply don't know you offer food. Whatever the reason, put people first. They are still paying for the entertainment portion of your facility. If they have a good time, they will keep coming back. And they will most likely figure out your outside food policy before their third visit.

Having established that our focus should be on the customer, let's discuss how to *Do More* with Service Resolution. The three skills are to *exceed expectations*, offer something *extra*, and *evaluate* your customer service performance.

Exceed Expectations

Whenever possible, *Do More* to show the guest that you are sorry and that you really care about their challenge. A great way to *exceed their expectations* is to thank them for informing you of the situation. This is how you let them know that you are serious about keeping their business. For every customer who complains, there are around twenty-four more[10] that have experienced the same problem and never said anything. So show gratitude to them for bringing the challenge to your attention; it really is a gift they are giving you.

Extra

In the case of Service Resolution, doing something *extra* means that you check back with the customer. At an appropriate moment after the challenge has been resolved, follow-up with the guest. Ask how the resolved challenge is working for them. Let them know that you sincerely care and are willing (happy to help) to do anything else necessary to ensure that the challenge is completely resolved and any errors have been corrected. A great way to determine your success is to simply ask them.

Evaluate

Next, you will want to make a record of the transaction, service gap, and resolution for the customer. Archive or document the challenge to avoid future problems and track possible recurring incidents. This will help you see trends where service is lacking, prevent it from happening to other guests, and allow you to evaluate if the challenge has really been resolved. If the same challenge continues, then you may need to *evaluate* your training, processes, or systems to see what may be causing the service gap.

Empowerment (*Bonus skill for Service Resolution*)

Your employees shouldn't only be *empowered* to fix things for your customer, they should be allowed to go above and beyond to *exceed expectations* for your customer in creating Service Resolution.

For effective Service Recovery, always put yourself in your customer's shoes and treat them as you would like to be treated. Better yet, treat them as *they* would like to be treated! Your customers are your most valuable asset. There is a great quote about customer service that says, "A satisfied guest will tell five people about their experience, a dissatisfied guest will tell anyone who will listen." Remember what Professor Dewar said? "Stories about your service failures get juicier and worse every time they are told. You can never win a storytelling contest with a customer."[11] Do your best to ensure that the tales are getting extra juicy about your excellent service, rather than negative experiences.

Barlow and Maul found that the best service providers keep their customers nearly fifty percent longer than other competitors.[12] In addition, ninety-five percent of complaining customers will give you another chance if you resolve their problem.[13]

Let's see how some organizations have handled Service Resolution. Raylene recently traveled from Utah to North Dakota to be with her daughter during the holidays as well as the arrival of a new baby. She explains what happened in her own words:

"Okay, so I started using my Capital One Visa. Well, I'd received an email over a week before my trip that they'd mailed me a new card. [But] it hadn't yet arrived in Utah.

"So I called the company and was able to talk to someone right away. The representative on the phone said she'd send me a new card and close down the old one. But she had it closed before she had even finished telling me her plan.

"'WHAT!?? What am I going to use now?' I fretted.

"She couldn't open it back up, so she transferred me to someone else. The new representative ordered a new card for me with 1.5% cash back, no annual fee, no foreign fee, and sent it two-day shipping through FedEx for me.

"She called yesterday to check to see if it had arrived yet, while I was holding the new baby who was being noisy.

"'Do you need anything else while I'm on the line?' she asked.

"'No, thank you and have a great Christmas!' I responded.

"Amazing service! But that's not all.

"I just received a big box. In it was a beautiful baby gift basket with towels embroidered with monkeys, a bear blanket, alligator wash-cloths, and a stuffed monkey on top.

"WOW! They win the prize for best customer service and best credit card!"[14]

The woman with Capital One who helped Raylene, not only solved her problem, but went above and beyond to show her that she really cares about having a business relationship with Raylene.

The second example occurred one evening while I was working at the bowling center. I heard someone shout, "Parker needs a raise!"

"He just got one!" was my quick reply, and it was also the truth. Nonetheless, it was clear to see that this guest had received some excellent service, and felt that the service provider deserved some compensation.

As the evening went on, I made my rounds talking to guests. When I arrived at this customer's table, she mentioned again that she and her friends thought that Parker was amazing and actually needed a raise. She also mentioned a bad experience they'd had the last time that they had come to our facility. I grabbed some paper and explained that I would like to document her situation to use in future training courses. Her story follows.

Approximately one year earlier, Lisa and a couple of friends came to the bowling center. The desk attendant was not very pleasant or en-thusiastic, and in fact was downright rude. She explained at one point he said, "You don't even need to be here."

Despite the bad service they had received, Lisa and her friends decided to give the place another chance. They came back about a week later and the same employee was working. He was still being unenthu-siastic and rude. When she and her friend had issues with their lane, he was rude about fixing them and even accused the group of causing the issue. Later, when they had another issue with their lane, the employee completely ignored their request for help, and let the issue go unresolved until the group finally left. The experience was such that Lisa and her friends knew they would not be back for a long time.

It was about a year before Lisa decided to return. Her first return visit occurred about one week before I had the opportunity to meet with her. She explained that she and her friends were pleasantly surprised with the service that Parker gave them. She explained that, "Parker was friendly, energetic, and seemed genuinely happy to be helping us" (her own words, not mine). "He was even enthusiastic about fixing problems on our lanes. He gave us great service." She explained that when he was unable to fix the problem on their bowling lane immediately, he moved them to another lane. As the group was leaving, he offered them some free game passes for the inconvenience.

Parker made such an impression on Lisa and her friends that they not only returned the very next week, but brought six friends with them, for a total of ten guests.[15] Parker's great guest service and skillful Service Resolution showed instant results, including increases in revenue, a growing customer family, and repeat visits to the facility.

Happy to Help   Service Resolution

Do More – Revisited

Bryce has been asked by his company to start a new training program. He receives the parameters from the VP of his department and begins looking for the program that he believes will best suit his organization. After finding that program, he attends the course, and receives certification to train that course in his organization.

As he prepares to train his first course, he goes online to order materials. When the materials arrive just a few days before training, he sees that they are not the materials he needs for his course, so he calls the support number for resolution.

Discover/Engage: "Thanks for calling Business Training Associates. This is Jeff. How can I help you today?" a voice asks enthusiastically.

Bryce explains, "I recently went through your certification and will be training in a couple of days. My materials arrived, but they don't seem to be the materials that I ordered."

Discover/Enquire: Jeff asks for Bryce's information and finds his profile on the company's account management system. "I see here that you placed an order for Product X, is that correct?"

"That is correct, but I opened up the packages you shipped, and it's all Product Y," Bryce replies.

Discover/Empathy: "Wow, I'm really sorry about that," Jeff explains. "Let's see what we can do to get this resolved for you."

"That would be great!" Bryce says enthusiastically.

Deliver/Exactly: Bryce hears keys being punched on the keyboard, and Jeff explains that he is re-entering the order.

Deliver/Elegantly: "Thank you so much for your patience," Jeff says. "It will just take me a minute to re-enter this order properly."

Deliver/Energetically: "Alright!" Jeff exclaims. "I think we've got your order all set-up here. Let me confirm this order and verify the quantity you need of Product X.

Do More/Exceed Expectations: Jeff also explains that he will have the product shipped over night, free of charge, to ensure that Bryce has what he needs in time. Bryce asks if he should send back what he received.

Do More/Empowerment: Jeff explains Bryce can ship back the product he doesn't need and Jeff will credit the amount spent on shipping charges to Bryce's account for his next purchase.

Do More/Evaluate: Following the phone call, Jeff logs into the company's account management system about the issue. He sends a note to the warehouse to create visibility, and the opportunity to double-check their orders.

Do More/Extra: The next day, Jeff calls Bryce to confirm that the order arrived and that the correct product was received. He sends Bryce free posters that the organization usually charges for, that can be used during Bryce's training.

Summary

The same steps that apply to offering great customer service apply to creating Service Resolution. *Discover* what the service gap was by *engaging* the customer and again *enquiring* about their needs. Apologize for the problem and *enlighten* them as to what will be done to create Service Resolution. *Deliver* their needs or fix the problem *exactly* as requested. Remain *elegant* and *energetic* throughout the entire experience. Let them know that you want to create Service Resolution and keep their business.

Do More by making it up to your customer. *Exceed their expectations* with the solution that you offer. Thank them for bringing the issue to your attention. Do something *extra* by checking back with them and ensuring that everything has been resolved to standard. *Evaluate* your performance and document the situation to prevent future service gaps of the same type from occurring. Using the skills of *Discover*, *Deliver*, and *Do More* for Service Recovery will help you to maintain great relationships and grow a thriving business community and customer family.

Review

Here are some more questions to help get some discussion going about how you are creating Service Resolution for your guests.

- Who do your customers typically go to first when they are seeking Service Resolution?
- Is this person trained and *empowered* to solve customer challenges?
- Are any of your team members trained or expected to resolve service challenges?
- How are customer challenges currently handled?
- Can the process for Service Resolution be improved? If so, in what ways?
- Do you currently have a process for tracking customer service challenges?
- What are issues that may occur frequently i.e., things that often cause customer challenges?
- Are there parts of your setting or systems that can be modified to improve performance and *Delivery*?
- What are things that can be done to *exceed* your customer's *expectations* after resolving an issue?
- Are all employees empowered to offer *extras*?
- What is your company currently doing to track guest satisfaction?

Exercises

1. With a learning partner, work through an entire transaction. You will act as a customer, while your learning partner acts as an employee. You, as the customer, should act as if it is your first time purchasing from the business. Assume that there has been a gap in service that must now be resolved. Allow the employee to *Discover, Deliver,* and *Do More* to create Service Resolution.

2. After finishing the entire transaction, switch roles. Run through the scenario again, but make sure that your learning partner, who is now the customer, experiences a different service gap. Utilize the skills you've learned to create Service Resolution.

3. After you have finished this second transaction, make a list of the following:

    a. Common ways to effectively *Discover* more about your customer's issue.

    b. Prime opportunities to *Deliver* the Service Resolution needs of your customer.

    c. Specific ways you can *Do More* to impress your customer and build loyalty while creating Service Resolution.

4. Now go through two more transactions, each of you with an opportunity to be the customer again. This time each of you will pose as a loyal customer who purchases from your business often.

5. After these two transactions, make a list of common ways to *Discover, Deliver,* and *Do More* to create Service Resolution for a loyal customer who has experienced a gap in service.

6. Compare the two lists you have now created, one from a first-time customer and one from a loyal repeat customer. Discuss the following:
    a. What is the same about how you create Service Resolution for a new customer versus an existing one?
    b. What is different?
    c. What would be the most important thing to train a new employee about fixing service gaps to create Service Resolution?
7. Share what you've learned with a minimum of three coworkers.

Extra Credit

This extra credit assignment requires a service gap before you can compare with your own organization. The next time you witness a service gap at another business, observe how the competition compares to your own organization.

EASY: Regarding Service Recovery, what do you do at your organization that is better than other businesses?

INTERMEDIATE: Regarding Service Recovery, what do you and other organizations do about the same? What can you do to differentiate your organization from your competitors?

HARD: Regarding Service Recovery, what have you seen other companies do better than your organization? What needs to happen for your organization to take Service Recovery to the next level?

Worth a Thousand Words

Which of these would you want to complain to if you had a service gap?

Hint: One poster directs you to speak to a manager, which is no promise of resolution. The other promises to make it right.

CUSTOMER SERVICE
PERFORMANCE 101

Not every customer interaction will be a dazzling relationship like the one I had with my favorite server, Reno. It won't be always be like the relationship I had with Brian who brought so many people into the bowling alley. So what do you do for everyone else? Here are a plethora of things that employees can reference to *Do More* on a regular basis. It is much easier for a new hire to process, "Try to do at least one thing off of this list for each person who you interact with today" rather than, "Master every single one of these, right now." You and your organization can use each of these as strategies to build relationships and offer better Customer Service Performance.

Mindset

1. Pay attention to customer service wherever you go. Learn new tips, tricks, and tactics for building relationships and improving performance.

2. Read a book about customer service (besides this one).

3. Google a term like *Customer Service*, *Customer Retention*, or *Customer Experience*. Read the first three search results.

4. Tell someone about what you learned from a book you read or the Google search.

5. Take a few moments to define and understand your own service vision. Evaluate how your personal vision fits into your organizations professional vision.

Before

6. Use your product so you can understand how it works and how customers will use it. This will also help you to make personal recommendations for your customer.

7. Listen to your favorite song before work to get you excited and ready to work with your customer family.

8. Watch cat videos to put you in a good mood.

9. Read Chuck Norris jokes.

10. If none of the three previous strategies work for you, find the inspiration for whatever makes you happy and excited before starting your shift. Apply as necessary.

11. Learn a new skill to create better experiences for your guests. Let them know that you learned something special specifically to help them.

12. You only get one chance to make a great first impression. Each day, evaluate what your customer's first impression of you will be.

13. Don't make your customer wait for you. You should always be waiting to help them when they are ready. If you see that a customer is waiting for you, evaluate what you can do differently to not make them, or others, wait in the future.

14. Put your mobile phone away. It should never be out, or someplace that it will tempt you, in a customer-facing space.

15. De-stress during breaks so you can always be your best self for the next guest.

16. Learn how to effectively use your company's customer relationship management system.

17. Be on time.

18. Dress appropriately for your role. Regardless of the dress code, always look your best.

19. Train, train, train. Then practice, practice, practice. Maximizing customer service performance is a process, not an event. Review the practice exercises in this book.

During

20. Smile at every customer you interact with.

21. Similar to number 12 (be ready when your customer is ready), give a customer as much time as they need to decide and/or order. Don't rush them.

22. Learn your customers' names. Remember them and use them often.

23. Offer a sincere compliment to your customer.

24. Learn about one of your customers' preferences. Remember it the next time you see them.

25. Tell an appropriate joke (something you'd be comfortable telling around your grandmother).

26. Give them something for free for being a loyal customer.

(However, don't use this strategy to entice a new customer to do business with you.)

27. Find out when your customer's birthday is and do something to recognize it.

28. Learn something new about your customer. Refer to it later.

29. Help with small children.

30. Do a magic trick.

31. Say *please*.

32. Say *thank you*.

33. Say *you're welcome*.

34. Learn about what they do for a job and be interested in their skills.

35. If your customer needs something and you can't help them, suggest a competitor who can.

36. Ask a customer why they prefer you over a competitor. Share what you learn with a coworker.

37. Make an exception. Just for them, just this one time.

38. Make eye contact.

39. Train your customer. The next customer who doesn't understand a process or policy, try to help them clearly understand why that policy is in place. Saying, "That's our policy," isn't good enough.

40. Show, don't tell. When someone asks where something is, don't just tell them where it is, show it to them.

41. If for some reason you can't show it to them, point appropriately. In some cultures, it is rude to point with a single finger. Use two fingers or motion with your whole hand.

42. Answer questions with more than one word.

43. Find something you have in common.

44. Avoid using industry jargon, slang, and acronyms.

45. The next time you say something that seems to confuse a customer,

think back to that later and evaluate if there is a way to explain it more clearly. Like the "Three games for eight dollars" example.

46. If you have a process that prevents you from taking your customers' money in certain scenarios, explore why the process is in place. If you can, change it.

47. Encourage suggestions from customers.

48. Give your undivided attention. If you are helping a customer, have someone else answer the phone whenever possible.

49. Get together with management and coworkers and create a list of ways to exceed the expectations of your customer that everyone is approved to do.

50. Recognize when you need additional help. Don't be afraid to ask for it.

51. Recognize first time customers. *Celebritize* them. Treat them like they are the best thing to happen to you that day (because they are).

52. Listen without interruption.

53. If you have to leave a customer, let them know what you're doing and how long it will take.

54. When you can't help a customer, suggest a good alternative. I once had a friend ask a server for a lime in his soda. She said she didn't have lime, but could do a lemon. He was satisfied not just with the lemon, but with how she anticipated his need.

55. Double-check every order. Read it back to your customer or summarize their needs.

56. Acknowledge every customer.

57. Only help one customer at a time.

58. As customers leave, or you finish an interaction with them, thank them for their business.

After

59. Write a thank-you card.

60. Offer them benefits for being loyal and coming back, not for being new.

61. Don't complain about your customers. Ever.

62. Pay attention to customer service wherever you go. Learn new tips, tricks, and tactics for building relationships and improving performance. You're right! It is in this list twice—that's because it is REALLY important.

63. Be willing to learn from the great habits of others. Observe a good habit that one of your coworkers does that you don't. Talk with them to learn about how you can make it a good habit.

64. Evaluate yourself and set measurable goals to continuously improve e.g., what percentage of customers are you thanking for their business?

65. Evaluate your customer service experience from your customer's perspective. Make a list of things you think could be done better and share it with your coworkers.

Service Resolution

66. If you have to fix a service gap, always let them know what you are going to do to fix it and create Service Resolution.

67. When someone complains, let them do all the talking.

68. Put yourself in their shoes. If you had been in their situation, how would you want someone to treat you and resolve the problem?

69. Respond to complaints as quickly as possible. The timing will vary depending on your industry—obviously face-to-face would be immediate. But even over the phone or email, you should be able to respond within four business hours.

70. Respond to every complaint.

71. Follow-up after you have resolved the issue to ensure that every-thing was resolved to their standard.

Not Face-to-Face

72. Tell your customer your name as soon as possible.

73. Smile when you answer the phone. Put a mirror next to it so you can see your face each time.

74. As soon as a customer mentions their name, write it down or enter it into your account management system so you don't have to ask for it again.

75. Hang a picture in your work area of something that makes you happy.

76. If you have to put a customer on hold, let them know what you are doing and how long it will take.

77. If it will take you more than eight business hours to respond to an email, let them know.

78. Verify phone numbers and email addresses.

79. Begin emails with salutations and close them with a personalized signature.

80. Write messages as you would say them.

81. User proper grammar and spelling.

82. Thank your customer for the opportunity to work with them.

Teamwork

83. Praise your co-workers. Don't belittle or make fun of them. Avoid gossip about them to other co-workers or customers.

84. Treat coworkers as you would a customer and vice versa.

85. Collaborate with a coworker to determine one another's strengths

and weaknesses in regard to customer service. Make goals for improvement and hold each other accountable.

86. Take time every day to share a positive customer experience with a coworker. Do this as a team for at least fifteen minutes every week.

Setting

87. Unless it is a very deliberate part of your performance, your facility should be neat, clean, and sanitary (I once went to a pirate-themed restaurant, it was supposed to look dirty). Pick up any trash that you see on the floor. Straighten things out and tidy up when you can.

88. Restrooms are your lowest common denominator. They need to be cleaned, **often**.

89. Some organizations don't allow vacuuming while customers are present. If this is the case, then just wait until you've closed. It looks better then turning off and hiding the vacuum when people arrive.

For Managers

90. Reward great service providers. Reward even the small wins. One of the best rewards is plain and simple recognition.

91. Measure your customer service performance. Evaluate weak areas and strive to make them better.

92. Measure continually to see if you are improving.

93. Before running a marketing campaign to grow revenue, consider how you can leverage your existing customer base. Can you get them to purchase more often, and in larger quantities with each purchase?

94. Ask front-line employees what processes should change. If they

want a change, have them propose a plan for how to make the improvement.

95. Compare yourself to the competition, often.

96. Incentivize as a team. Friendly competition is only fun for the winners. If it's always the same person winning, then there is a problem with the contest.

97. Reward behaviors as well as results.

98. Determine the value of each customer and each transaction. Share that number with every employee.

Always

99. Remember that the best PR is Personal Recommendations.

100. Have fun. A lot of fun.

101. Smile till you mean it!

CONCLUSION

The argument could be made that bad, mediocre, and even average customer service is the result of employees that aren't motivated to offer great service. That may be partly true, but having the skills to do what is necessary is a larger part of motivating someone. How motivated are you to do something if you don't even know how to do it?

Recently, I visited a large retail store. Things seemed a little busier than normal. This became even more apparent when I noticed an employee in a reflective vest cashiering in the checkout lane where I was waiting to be served. I presumed he was one of the cart wranglers, but, due to the busyness of the day, was called inside to work a checkout line. I could see the frustration and exasperation on his face. When a manager walked by, the checker mumbled something that I couldn't hear. The manager replied with something like, "Don't worry, it will slow down in a little bit." In short, this young man did not like checking out or dealing with customers, yet was working as a cashier in a retail store!

Another recent experience occurred when I was eating at a Subway. It was a little slower that day, and I commented on how slow it was. One of the employees commented that he likes it better when it's busier. I asked if that was because things go faster that way.

He responded, "Well, yeah. That, too. Mostly I just love my customers. I like being able to help them and take care of them."

I appreciate this attitude and wish that there were more people out there giving service like this young man. The difference between these two individuals is that one doesn't know how to (and so doesn't care to) help his customers, while the other is always happy to help.

Customers can be gained, maintained, and retained, revenues will be increased, and employees will be happier working in a service atmosphere following the simple skills, steps, and strategies included in this book.

- *Discover* your guest's needs by *engaging* them in casual conversation, *enquiring* about their needs and expectations, and *enlightening* them about your systems and processes.
- *Deliver exactly* what your guest asked for. Be sure that you do it *elegantly*, being pleasant and polite. *Deliver energetically* to create a better customer service experience.
- *Do More* for your guest by finding ways to *exceed expectations*. They don't need to be HUGE to be effective. Some things will happen around the time of the transaction. Other *extras* may take place later but can still show your customer that you care. Whenever

possible, *evaluate* your performance to see where improvements need to be made and where successes occurred.

In regard to service gaps, utilize *Discover, Deliver, Do More* to create Service Resolution. In these situations, *empowerment* is a must in being able to fix problems for a customer. Remember, always apologize about the service gap and *empathize* with your customer as you work to create Service Resolution.

You will see employees who learn to be happy to help their customers, and become happy to help everyone else as well. You can recognize these people because they follow the steps outlined in this book in their own lives.

During a period of my own unemployment, my family was the recipient of a Secret Santa gift. Whoever the Secret Santa was *Discovered* and *Delivered* the needs of our family. They *Did More* and went the extra mile by discretely learning about each of our children's interests. Each child received a personalized gift.

When leaving the office where I worked for lunch, my truck wouldn't start. I had someone help me try to jump start it but to no avail. When I went back into the office to ask if one of the guys with a bigger truck could tow me to the shop, one of them jumped into action. It turns out he was a mechanic before he became an account representative for our company. But he didn't just *Discover* what was wrong, and then *Deliver* by telling me how to fix it. He was willing to *Do More* and drove me to the nearest Auto Zone where he showed me what to purchase, and then helped me replace the part in my truck.

I was chatting with my neighbor and mentioned that I liked his tie. He took it off and gave it to me. I was a little shocked, but later learned this is how he takes care of his customer family. My neighbor owns (or has owned) hundreds of ties. He works as a furniture salesman and is known as "The Tie Guy." Anytime anyone says they like his tie, he gives it to them. As in my case, I've seen him do it outside of work as well. It's not something he does just to be nice or to make the sale; it's a code he lives by.

Take these steps and apply them to your work and to your life. A customer can be anyone who is asking you to do any kind of service for them. You can maximize customer service performance, build relationships, and always be happy to help as you *Discover, Deliver*, and *Do More*. Use *Discover, Deliver* and *Do More* to:

❏ Ensure customer happiness and retention
❏ Increase spending with each transaction
❏ Accelerate the frequency of purchasing
❏ Multiply your customers' personal recommendations
❏ Experience an expanded and thriving customer family
❏ Continuously cultivate lasting loyal business relationships

Be good to your customer family.

WORKS CITED

Introduction

1. This is a story my grandparents often shared at family gatherings.

2. Gitomer, Jeffrey. *The Little Red Book of Sellin: 12.5 Principles of Sales Greatness: How to Make Sales Forever*. Bard Press, 2005, pp. 7.

3. Tschohl, John. "Companies Don't See Reality in Their Service Reflection." Service Quality Institute, 21 Mar. 2013, http://www.customer-service.com/blog/201303/companies_misunderstand_what_customers_want

4. Weinzwig, Ari. *Zingerman's Guide to Giving Great Service*. Hyperion, 2003, pp. 72-73.

5. Khalsa, Mahan. *Let's Get Real or Let's Not Play: The Demise of Dysfunctional Selling and the Advent of Helping Clients Succeed*. White Water Press, 1999, pp. 28.

6. Baer, Jay. *Hug Your Haters*. Portfolio / Penguin, 2016, pp. 23.

7. White, Randy. "Back to the Basics: The Only Five Ways to Grow Your Business." Leisure eNewsletter, Vol. XIV, No. 2, February-March 2014, https://www.whitehutchinson.com/news/lenews/2014_march/article107.shtml

8. Ibid.

9. Ibid.

10. Whitler, Kimberly. "Why Word of Mouth Marketing Is The Most Important Social Media." Forbes, 17 Jul. 2014, https://www.forbes.com/sites/kimberlywhitler/2014/07/17/why-word-of-mouth-marketing-is-the-most-important-social-media

Discover

1. Alex: Personal interviews with the author, 2013. The first scenario and the "Revisited" scenario happened to different people at the same store. They were combined under one pseudonym to compare the different service experiences.

2. Lacy: Personal interview with the author, 2012.

3. Portnoy, Gary, and Judy Hart Angelo. Performed by Gary Portnoy. *Where Everybody Knows Your Name*. Featured as the theme song on an American sitcom called Cheers, which aired on television in syndication from 1982 to 1993.

4. Carnegie, Dale. *How to Win Friends & Influence People*. Gallery Books, 1936, pp. 79.

5. Blanchard, Ken, and Sheldon Bowles. Raving Fans: *A Revolutionary Approach to Customer Service*. William Morrow and Company, Inc., 1993, pp. 111.

6. Weinzwig, Ari. *Zingerman's Guide to Giving Great Service*. Hyperion, 2003, pp. 39-40.

7. Cammie: Personal interview with the author, 2015.

8. Oches, Sam. "The 2016 QSR Drive-Thru Study." QSR, Oct. 2016, https://www.qsrmagazine.com/reports/2016-qsr-drive-thru-study

9. Connellan, Tom. *Inside the Magic Kingdom: Seven Keys to Disney's Success*. Bard Press, 1997, pp. 75.

10. Nicholas: Personal interview with the author, 2014.

11. Sabrina: Personal interview with the author, 2014.

12. Sheridan, Rich. *Joy, Inc.* Portfolio / Penguin, 2013, pp. 77.

13. Chad: Personal interview with the author, 2016.

Deliver

1. Tim: Personal interviews with the author, 2011. The first scenario and the "Revisited" scenario happened to different people at similar restaurants. They were combined under one pseudonym to compare the different service experiences.

2. Schultz, Howard. "Starbucks CEO Howard Schultz is All abuzz." CBS News, 5 Jun. 2012, http://www.cbsnews.com/news/starbucks-ceo-howard-schultz-is-all-abuzz/.

3. Chase: Personal interview with the author, 2015.

4. Disney Institute. *Be Our Guest: Perfecting the art of customer service*. Disney Editions, New York, 2001, pp. 109-10.

5. Brett: Personal interview with the author, 2010.

6. Barlow, Janelle, and Dianna Maul. *Emotional Value: Creating Strong Bonds With Your Customers*. Berret-Kohler Publishers, Inc., 2000, pp. 6.

7. Baer, Jay. *Hug Your Haters*. Portfolio / Penguin, 2016, pp. 28.

8. Weinzwig, Ari. *Zingerman's Guide to Giving Great Service*. Hyperion, 2003, pp. 44-45.

9. Pine II, Joseph B., and James H Gilmore. *The Experience Economy*. Harvard Business School Press, 1999.

10. Price, Frank. Price said this during a training for family entertainment center owners and operators during his training, *Birthday University*, during a convention of the International Association of Amusement Parks and Attractions (IAAPA), Atlanta, Georgia, Nov. 2006.

11. *Mary Poppins*. Based on the "Mary Poppins" books by P. L. Travers, directed by Robert Stevenson, screenplay by Bill Walsh, performance by Julie Andrews, Walt Disney, 1964

12. Brandon: Personal interview with the author, 2016.

Do More

1. Jackie: Personal interviews with the author, 2012. The first scenario and the "Revisited" scenario happened to different people at the entertainment venue. They were combined under one pseudonym to compare the different service experiences.

2. White, Randy. "Back to the Basics: The Only Five Ways to Grow Your Business." Leisure eNewsletter, Vol. XIV, No. 2, February-March 2014, https://www.whitehutchinson.com/news/lenews/2014_march/article107.shtml

3. Tschohl, John. "Companies Don't See Reality in Their Service Reflection." Service Quality Institute, 21 Mar. 2013, http://www.customer-service.com/blog/201303/companies_misunderstand_what_customers_want

4. Performance Research Associates, Inc. *Delivering Knock Your Socks Off Service: 20th Anniversary Edition*. American Management Association, 2012, pp. 50-52.

5. Roscoe: Personal interview with the author, originally posted on Facebook, 14 December 2016.

6. Heather: Personal interview with the author, 2016.

7. Hyken, Shep. *The Amazement Revolution: Seven Customer Service Strategies to Create an Amazing Customer (and Employee Experience)*. Greenleaf Book Group Press, 2011, pp. 1.

8. Rob and Laura: Personal interview with the author, 2013.

9. Gross, T. Scott. *Positively Outrageous Service*. Dearborn Trade Publishing, 2004, 12-13.

10. Sean: Personal interview with the author, 2015.

11. Gross, T. Scott. *Why Service Stinks…And Exactly What to Do About It!* Dearborn Trade Publishing, 2004, pp. 13.

12. Pine II, Joseph B., and James H Gilmore. *The Experience Economy*. Harvard Business School Press, 1999, pp. 136.

Service Resolution

1. Bryce: Personal interviews with the author, 2016. The first scenario is fictitious, while the "Revisited" scenario really happened. This first scenario was created as a view of how things could have gone wrong in a similar situation.

2. Reichheld, Frederick F., and W. Earl Sasser Jr. "Zero Defections: Quality Comes to Services." *Harvard Business Review*. Oct. 1990.

3. Goodman, John A. *Customer Experience 3.0: High Profit Strategies in the Age of Techno Service*. American Management Association, 2014, pp. 24.

4. Gross, T. Scott. *Why Service Stinks….And Exactly What to Do About It!* Dearborn Trade Publishing, 2004, pp. 165-67.

5. Dewar, Robert D. "Customer Relations Under Fire." *Best of Class: Building a Customer Service Organization*. Edited by Ken Shelton, Executive Excellence Publishing, 1998.

6. Weinzwig, Ari. *Zingerman's Guide to Giving Great Service*. Hyperion, 2003, pp. 59-60.

7. Grenny, Joseph. "It's Not Poor Customer Service, It's Silence That Costs You." Crucial Skills, 10 Nov. 2015, https://www.vitalsmarts.com/crucialskills/2015/11/its-not-poor-customer-service-its-silence-that-costs-you/.

8. Baer, Jay. *Hug Your Haters*. Portfolio / Penguin, 2016, pp. 28.

9. Winch, Guy. *The Squeaky Wheel: Complaining the Right Way to Get Results, Improve Your Relationships, and Enhance Self-Esteem*. Walker Publishing Company, Kindle edition, 2011.

10. Baer, Jay. *Hug Your Haters*. Portfolio / Penguin, 2016, pp. 28.

11. Dewar, Robert D. "Customer Relations Under Fire." *Best of Class: Building a Customer Service Organization*. Edited by Ken Shelton, Executive Excellence Publishing, 1998.

12. Barlow, Janelle, and Dianna Maul. *Emotional Value: Creating Strong Bonds With Your Customers*. Berret-Kohler Publishers, Inc., 2000.

13. Timm, Paul R. "Use the Profit Power of Customer Service." *Best of Class: Building a Customer Service Organization.* Edited by Ken Shelton, Executive Excellence Publishing, 1998.

14. Raylene: Personal interview with the author, originally posted on Facebook, 14 Dec. 2016.

15. Lisa: Personal interview with the author, 2011.

ABOUT THE AUTHOR

Jesse B. Good is an enthusiastic presenter, skilled communica-
tor, and customer service expert. With over two decades of hands-on,
front-line expertise, he has facilitated more than one million customer
service experiences. He delivers dynamic speeches and memorable
training courses based on twenty years of on-going research. These tools
help organizations effectively train, maintain, and sustain maximized
service performance; drive rapid, sustainable, and measureable change in
customer experiences; and cultivate client relationships that dramatically
improve business results.

Jesse lives in Utah with his wife Lacy, and their seven children.